In the Best Interest of the Child

AN EVALUATION OF ASSESSMENT CENTERS

Other Pergamon titles of interest

G. Cartledge & J. F. Milburn
Teaching Social Skills to Children

O. K. Garnica & M. L. King
Language, Children and Society

J. H. Kahn et al.
Unwillingly to School, 3rd edition

J. H. Kahn & S. E. Wright
Human Growth and the Development of Personality, 3rd edition

P. B. Mrazek & C. H. Kempe
Sexually Abused Children and their Families

S. Schwartz & J. H. Johnson
Psychopathology of Childhood

A Related Journal*

Children and Youth Services Review
An International Multidisciplinary Quarterly Review of the
Welfare of Young People

Coordinating Editor: D. Lindsey, Washington University, Missouri

This Review encourages research from various sources to be focused
on programs and policies to support the welfare of children and
youth. The journal serves as a multidisciplinary meeting ground
for the highest standards of critical and considered inquiry into the
issues and service programs affecting children and seeks a
confluence of science and humanities in the area of child welfare.
Evaluation studies of service programs are particularly encouraged.
Topics include such issues as childrens' rights, day care programs,
youth employment programs, and studies of institutions serving
children and youth.

*Free specimen copy available on request.

In the Best Interest of the Child

AN EVALUATION OF ASSESSMENT CENTERS

by

JERRY JACOBS

Professor of Sociology
Syracuse University, New York

PERGAMON PRESS
OXFORD · NEW YORK · TORONTO · SYDNEY · PARIS · FRANKFURT

U.K.	Pergamon Press Ltd., Headington Hill Hall, Oxford OX3 0BW, England
U.S.A.	Pergamon Press Inc., Maxwell House, Fairview Park, Elmsford, New York 10523, U.S.A.
CANADA	Pergamon Press Canada Ltd., Suite 104, 150 Consumers Rd., Willowdale, Ontario M2J 1P9, Canada
AUSTRALIA	Pergamon Press (Aust.) Pty. Ltd., P.O. Box 544, Potts Point, N.S.W. 2011, Australia
FRANCE	Pergamon Press SARL, 24 rue des Ecoles, 75240 Paris, Cedex 05, France
FEDERAL REPUBLIC OF GERMANY	Pergamon Press GmbH, 6242 Kronberg-Taunus, Hammerweg 6, Federal Republic of Germany

First edition 1982

Library of Congress Cataloging in Publication Data
Jacobs, Jerry.
In the best interest of the child.
1. Greater London Council. Assessment Center.
I. Title. [DNLM: 1. Community mental health centers—
London. 2. Personality assessment—In infancy and
childhood. WM 30 J175i]
HV752.L7J3   1981   362.7'4   81-17931
AACR2

British Library Cataloguing in Publication Data
Jacobs, Jerry
In the best interest of the child.
1. Children—Institutional care—London
I. Title
362.7'32'09421   HV887.G5
ISBN 0-08-028108-7

In order to make this volume available as economically and as rapidly as possible the typescript has been reproduced in its original form. This method unfortunately has its typographical limitations but it is hoped that they in no way distract the reader.

Printed in Great Britain by A. Wheaton & Co. Ltd., Exeter

Contents

1
House and Home:
An Overview

Under the terms of the 1971 reorganization of social services, the local authorities established children reception and assessment centers throughout England. These facilities serve to "receive and assess" children in trouble, i.e., delinquents, battered children, "school abstainers", run-aways, "incorrigibles", and the children of "unfit parents".

The following study will seek to understand how the staff at one of these centers sought to establish what was "in the best interest of the child". We will see who the childcare officers are, how they came by their jobs, their prior employment and background, the routine tasks associated with their work, the assessment process, their involvement in family therapy, their internal alliances and rivalries, and the state of their morale in light of the structural and personal changes currently confronting them. We will deal with the process of change that long-time members of staff experienced, and how newcomers confronted and were confronted by their immediate work environment. This then, will be the natural history of an English childcare center, and an attempt to account for how past events helped to create the present work situation described in the following chapters.

THE CENTER

The Assessment Center is located in London, and comprised of two separate units, Oxford and Cambridge. The former, because it housed the offices of the acting superintendent, became known as "headquarters". Staff conferences, intra- or inter-house business and the children's assessments were all staged there. Keeping in mind its administrative importance, we will begin our discussion with a description of Oxford.

Oxford

Oxford is located in council housing, and is composed of a
number of converted flats. Initially there was provision for
a fourteen-bed facility to be housed on four floors — eight
children on the third, and six on the fourth. A few years ago
a child set fire to the top floor, and while no one was injured,
the badly damaged sector was never reopened. (It was soon
after this that the original superintendent suffered a nervous
breakdown and resigned.) This reduced the number of children
from fourteen to eight. Notwithstanding the horror of the fire,
the staff and consultants feel that the child who set the fire
actually "did them all a favor" by increasing the staff-to-child
ratio and providing for the expansion of family therapy.

Currently, the unit is divided into three floors, each serving
a different purpose. The ground floor houses a small bathroom
for the children and locker area for the staff, the kitchen,
and a combination dining room and play area for the children.
This complex is the center of in-house activities. Most of the
children's and staff's waking hours are spent here. The
kitchen is separated in part from the dining room-play area by
a counter and hinged door. The door can be closed and locked
to provide a more permanent separation, but even then the area
appears, and is most often used as one large open space. Large
windows that open to the outside line the outer wall, giving
the entire area a light and airy feeling. A fenced backyard
is accessible through a door in the play room and serves as an
extension of the children's play area in good weather. The
dining area has two long tables placed end to end, with chairs
running the length of both sides. These are situated along the
inner wall farthest from the windows while a large black and
white television set and three stuffed chairs abut the outer
wall.

The kitchen houses all the accoutrements necessary for the
preparation of food for both the children and staff. Some of
this equipment was, however, in bad repair. For example, an
electric can opener had been broken for some time, and the
manual one worked only with difficulty. The latch to the oven
door had long been broken and would not stay closed, nor could
it be easily opened until it was repaired by the author.

The second floor contained two rooms that are used as the administrative offices, and a third and larger one where house meetings, administrative business, and the children's assessments are held. This area also serves as a time-out spot for the staff and is off limits to the children. It is one of the few places apart from the two offices where the staff could get away from the frequently hectic routine of the first floor. One of the offices, the one nearest the stairwell, serves as the administrative headquarters for the acting superintendent, and contains official house records and the children's case histories. A half-time administrative secretary (who is often 3/4 time without benefit of pay) also resides there. The offices and conference room which are strung in a row and are sparcely furnished have windows facing the street. At the head of the staircase is a small locked bedroom that is used by the night staff and considered off bounds to the children or other visitors.

The third floor contains the children's bedrooms. The two larger rooms house three children each, while the two smaller ones have single beds. The latter are reserved for the two older teenagers.

Toilets are located on the landing between the first and second floors. The bathrooms where the children received their daily baths are situated on the landing between the second and third floor. Finally, there is a small basement and storage area containing a laundry room, and a small locked pantry located on the landing between the basement and the first floor where the unit's provisions are stored. This interior, added to the stark brick exterior of the building, an exterior typical of council housing in working class neighborhoods, completes our description of Oxford.

Cambridge

Cambridge is a two-story brick building located in the same borough as Oxford and about a mile away. It too is situated in council housing, and from the outside, at least, the two units look alike. While viewed by its staff as the "step-child" of the Center, Cambridge was actually the older of the two, and first went into operation about 9 years ago. Oxford has only been operative for about 6 years.

Cambridge, because of its decor and architectural make-up, does
not have the homey feeling of Oxford. Like Oxford, the kitchen
and combination dining room — play and social area are on the
first floor along with a television set, some comfortable
chairs, and in a separate section of the room, dining room
tables and chairs. However, in the Cambridge floor plan the
kitchen is not an integral part of the dining room — play area,
and the staff office is located on the first floor, directly in
the traffic pattern. As a result, the kitchen is not quite as
central to social life as the one at Oxford; while the staff
office is not as isolated. In fact, the staff at Cambridge
have a difficult time in finding a place to get away from it all
since children are constantly coming into and out of the office
on one pretext or another.

This is true not only because of the location of the office,
but because of the differing age composition of the children.
It was the practice of the Center to place teenage children at
Cambridge, while Oxford catered to the pre-teen group. Apart
from the differing age cohort, there was the "looser", less
structured and generally more liberal care policies envoked by
the Cambridge staff, all of which contributed to a noisier and
more chaotic environment.

Rounding out the picture at Cambridge, the second floor housed
the children's bedrooms and bathrooms, and as at Oxford, a
locked bedroom for the nightstaff.

Grandview

There was for a period of time, late in the study, an unantici-
pated move on the part of Cambridge staff and children to a
third house, Grandview. This was required to give workmen time
to renovate Cambridge. However, the staff and children of
Cambridge, while they were required to move to Grandview, and
several weeks later back to Cambridge, were not to enjoy the
benefits of the renovation. Both houses, Cambridge and Oxford,
would within a couple of months be forced to move to a new and
larger facility called Queens Road; a move everyone, staff,
consultants, and children, were all opposed to. The effects of
this long anticipated move on in-house care and morale will be
the topic of detailed discussion in future chapters.

Because of the relatively minor part their stay at Grandview
played, at least in time, I will not go into a detailed description of this temporary housing arrangement. It is worthy of

note, however, that both staff and children found Grandview
very agreeable — superior to Cambridge, and far superior to the
"institutional" accommodations that awaited them at Queens Road.
This is not surprising given that the aim of the staff was to
make "a home" for the children within "a house". This job
would be made much easier if one had a house to start with, as
opposed to a structure that resembled a correctional facility.

ELIGIBILITY

As previously noted, children received and/or assessed by the
Center have generally been defined by the authorities as
requiring service. These include run-aways, battered children,
delinquent children, children with "school phobias", or those
who are a threat to themselves or others. Such children come
to the attention of the authorities in different ways. For
example, run-away minors are rounded up by the police in the
course of their daily routine and deposited at the Center "for
safekeeping". These children are frequently kept for only a
day or two and then sent home without being assessed. While
some children are only "received", others are "received" and
"assessed". For those being assessed, the case involves a
field social worker, who along with sundry other officials
acquire from a Magistrate a "remand order", putting the child
in the care of the Center for a specified period of time
(usually 6 weeks) for "observation and assessment". Here, the
house staff, in conjunction with outside consultants (psychiatrists and psychologists), seek to assess, on the basis of
their observations of the child, interviews with the family and
teachers, and all other relevant and involved parties, what is
"in the best interest of the child". Six weeks is rarely
viewed by staff or consultants as sufficient time to perform a
proper assessment and/or treatment, and "care orders" are sought
from the court that place the child in the custody of the Center
until the care order is rescinded, or until the child reaches
the age of 18. In fact, some of the children have been with
the Center for "assessment" for a year or more. The contradic-
tion of "extended care" within a "short-stay" home will be
considered in greater detail in later chapters.

THE CHILDCARE OFFICER

During their stay at the Center, children are under the direct
care and supervision of "childcare officers" (CCOs). We will
deal here only in a cursory way with this topic, since questions

of who the CCOs are, how they came by their job, their percep-
tions of their work, their qualifications, and on-the-job
benefits, will be dealt with in Chapter 2. Suffice it to say
at this point that it requires very little, if anything, in the
way of formal education or prior training to become a residential childcare officer. The level of training of the childcare
officers in this study, at the time of their first involvement
with the Center, ranged from zero to some working background
with children. In general, the workers' level of competence
upon first acquiring the job was uniformly very low by their
own admission. Their current formal "on-the-job training",
while it is considerable according to the civil service job
description bulletin, is almost nil, according to the workers.
"Play it by ear" and "osmose what you can" is the staff's
standard operating procedure as it relates to training.

THE CHILDREN

There are currently eight children housed at Oxford. While the
following sketches tell us something about them, a more detailed
discussion of some of their life histories will be presented in
Chapter 4.

Deborah is a 16-year-old girl who has been at Oxford for a total
of 18 months. She was placed in care as a result of "non-school
attendance", petty theft, "rejection by the mother" (abandonment)
and "out of control". She is from a working-class background,
talks and looks tough, smokes and curses a lot. The staff sees
her as cooperative and much improved as the result of her year
and a half stay at Oxford. Why has Deborah been at Oxford for
18 months instead of the 6 weeks a "remand order" usually runs?
Oxford was seen by the staff as the best of a bad situation for
Deborah, i.e., available living situations (as opposed to
recommended ones) were viewed as being even less "in her best
interest".

Falicia is a black 16-year-old girl who was at Oxford for only
about a week. She was committed to care because of a drug over-
dose, bad depression and suspected prostitution. Falicia had
a prior history at Oxford when a year earlier she and her boy-
friend were involved in a theft. This readmission was in no
way unusual. Many children were seen on a "revolving door"
basis.[1*] While at Oxford, Falicia threatened to kill herself,

_____

*Superscript numbers refer to Notes at end of book.

was "depressed" and "uncooperative". I noticed her absence
one day and inquired as to her whereabouts. While initially I
met with a wall of silence, it was later revealed that she had
cut her wrists and was brought to the hospital. While there
she refused psychiatric care, and after being returned to
Oxford "absconded".

Joan is a 12-year-old who has spent 12 months at Oxford. Prior
to that, she and a twin sister lived in a local children's
home. The mother accused the home of fostering lesbianism, and
Joan was removed to Oxford. She has been here since. She too
came from a working-class home, acted tough, cursed a lot,
openly rebelled against the staff, and rarely did as she was
asked. Most of the staff "had had it" with Joan and hoped she
would ultimately be moved elsewhere.

Nancy, age 12, and Alice, age 3½, are sisters who were committed
most recently to care about 4½ months ago when "the mother set
the house on fire". They were also admitted to Oxford about a
year ago as "battered children". They were currently being
assessed to decide whether or not to return them to their
parental home. Both children were beautiful, mischievous, and
the darlings of the house.

Peter is a 13-year-old boy who was admitted to the Center for
petty theft and "lack of school attendance". He, too, was
being assessed and has been there for a couple of months. He
was quiet, polite, and helpful, and like Nancy and Alice, came
from a lower working-class background. Indeed, the parents of
all these children were unemployed or marginally employed, and
had a long history of hard times.

Finally there were the three brothers, Noah, Joshua, and Jacob,
ages 6, 4, and 3½ respectively. These three black children had
been at the Center for assessment for about 2 months. The
parents had separated and the mother had battered the oldest of
the three. The children were admitted because it was felt that
they needed "care and protection".

Such was the background of some of the children at the Center
and the circumstances of their admission.

   THE ASSESSMENT PROCESS

A general overview of the assessment process reveals many of
the following features:

1. A "remand" or "care order" must be acquired from the courts.
2. A field social worker acting as a fact finding thera-peutic liaison between the family and Center is involved.
3. A psychiatric consultant (at this Center, at least) and one or more CCOs conduct a home interview with the parents and other relevant parties.
4. A psychological consultant does a series of psycho-logical tests to establish a personality profile of the child.
5. The CCOs in the course of their everyday duties discuss the child's behavior and affect at "handover" time, i.e., when staff comes on and goes off at different shifts.
6. Teachers, either in the regular school system, or those giving special tutorials, report on the child's progress in school.
7. There are case conferences involving staff, social workers, consultants, and parents.
8. There are one or more staff conferences, during which time inputs from all of these sources are discussed and considered, and the final assessment and recom-mendations regarding what is "in the best interest of the child" are made.
9. The "placement officer" assesses the availability of "real options".
10. These recommendations are forwarded to the court magistrate, who may abide by them or not as he sees fit.
11. Sometimes the Center's recommendations are contested by the parents in court actions.
12. Finally, there is some outcome and the child is "placed" either back in the family or in a care facility.

THE RECOMMENDATION

What are the range of possible alternatives available to the Center and the court regarding possible recommendations for a course of action on the child's behalf?

1. The child is returned to his/her parents, subject to certain constraints imposed by the court to insure the child's well-being, and to be monitored by the social worker.

2. The child is not returned to the unfit parents but is placed in a "long-term care facility".
3. The child is placed in a foster home.
4. The child is sent to a boarding school.
5. The child is placed in a special therapeutic setting.
6. Older children are placed in a training school.
7. Older teenagers (over 18) await placement in a "hostel".
8. The child remains for a relatively long stay at the Center.

This brief outline will be expanded and considered more extensively in Chapter 4. However, what has been presented thus far should serve for the time being to orient the reader for what is to come concerning the houses, how they work, who works there, who is worked upon, and the possible outcome for the child of all of these efforts.

2

The House Staff: Becoming a Childcare Officer

The house staff in both units are generally divided into two broad administrative categories — "junior" and "senior". There are many, however, who are very sensitive to any reference to "the hierarchy" and would like the distinction of junior and senior staff to be soft pedalled or eliminated entirely.

SENIOR AND JUNIOR STAFF

Among the first to espouse these sentiments was the top in-house upper echelon staff officer, the acting superintendent. Such a position is generally considered to be primarily administrative in nature. However, Sylvia (the acting superintendent for the past 3 years) spends more time with the children on the first floor than in her second floor office shuffling forms, letters, and billings. She has a sort of informal, rough, home-spun way while on the job, so that, as she herself has proudly said many times, newcomers to the house "can't tell the superintendent from the other staff". Ironically, and notwithstanding her direct home-spun approach with the lower echelon staff, the CCOs at both houses know her as someone who "rules with an iron fist". There is also widespread opinion that she is less than fair in her dealings; and that if one "gets on her wrong side" one is in for serious and sustained trouble. One CCO put it this way:

> "I've seen staff used and got rid of and this sort of thing
> in really horrible ways, and you know that things you
> (in staff meetings designed to air differences of opinion)
> are going to be used (against you) later on ... you say
> something and they pick that up as a sort of threat, and
> it's used later on. And I've known staff that were petri-
> fied of Sylvia... ."

Nor is the acting superintendent very interested in or capable
of record keeping or paper work. Notwithstanding all of this,
she is given by many at Oxford a great deal of respect. This
stems from two considerations: the popularity of her loose and
informal administration, and the high regard the staff has for
her, not as an administrator, but as a childcare officer. In
fact, her background is not unlike many of the children she
cares for; and she has not only a great deal of concern for
them and their problems, but a great deal of understanding as
well. With this in mind, it is perhaps not surprising to find
that it was only by accident that she acquired her present
position. Basically the position fell to her, on the basis of
seniority, when the prior superintendent was forced to resign.
She has always considered the position to be a sort of mixed
blessing. While gladly accepting the increase in status and
pay that went with her promotion, she only reluctantly accepted
her administrative duties. This was not through any lack of
industry on her part (she spent long hours at the Center, above
and beyond those required) but rather through a lack of interest
and/or competence. Much of the administrative running of the
Center was left to the part-time secretary. While it is in no
way unusual for administrators to delegate routine administrative tasks to their secretary, it was in this case perhaps
especially lucky. Her secretary, if she was not particularly
pleasant to deal with, was at least efficient and with a strong
sense of loyalty to her immediate superior.

Below the rank of superintendent there were two other senior
staff positions, one within each unit or house called "the
teamleader". Each "teamleader", or "head of house", had a
"deputy" or second in command. These and all other staff
(junior or senior) were ranked according to a system of rankings
within social services from grade 1 to 9, reflecting one's status
and income level. The following is a formal organization chart
indicating the current status hierarchy, and a second one illus-
trating how it will look after the move to Queens Road. This is
accompanied by a list of childcare officers at the Center, their
age and sex, and a staff status and income table. An interesting aside on this data is the fact that there were (apart from
the Black cook at Cambridge) no Blacks or ethnics employed by
the Center at any level.

Pay scales for childcare officers and domestics at the time of
the study have been noted below. One English pound was then
equivalent to U.S. $2. The cost of living in London is
frequently compared to the cost of living in New York City.
With this as a guideline, it is clear that childcare officers

supporting families are living at what would be defined in this country as a poverty level. It is perhaps not surprising to find that only three of the CCOs noted above were married and that only two (Alec and Shawn) had children.

The following in tabular form is the age and sex composition of the staff at Oxford and Cambridge.

OXFORD	Sex	Age
Digby (new superintendent)	M	44
Sylvia (old acting superintendent)	F	35
Judy	F	31
Alec	M	31
Ronald	M	28
Shawn	M	28
Meg	F	28
Cynthia	F	30
CAMBRIDGE		
Ann	F	31
Marilyn	F	29
Mary	F	25
Ian	M	22
Philip	M	22
Dinny	F	25

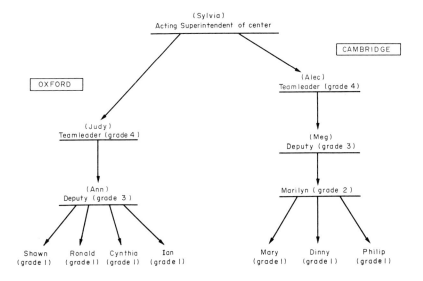

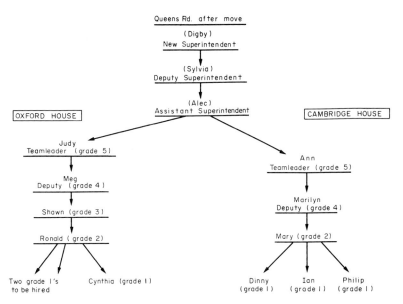

SPECIAL CLASSES OF OFFICERS

S.J.A.C. SCALES FOR STAFFS OF COMMUNITY HOMES WITH EFFECT FROM 1-7-75

Note: For London Weighting Allowances and Special London Allowance, see end of scales.

Note: All rates given below are in English pounds. One English pound is equivalent to two U.S. dollars.

GRADE 1	GRADE 2	GRADE 3	GRADE 4
1701	2277	2364	2607
1884	2364	2445	2691
1971	2445	2529	2775
2040	2529	2607	2853
2127	2607	2691	2922
2193	2691	2775	3009
2277 Responsibility Bar		2853	3096
2384			
2445			
2529			

GRADE 5	GRADE 5A	SENIOR GRADE
2775	2853	2607
2853	2922	2691
2922	3009	2775
3009	3096	2853
3096	3186	2922
3186	3282	3009
3282	3366	3096
3366	3474	3185
		3282 Qualification Bar
		3366
		3474
		3588
		3702
		3825
		3957

FOR RANGES 6-9A SEE NEXT PAGE

SPECIAL CLASSES OF OFFICERS
S.J.A.C. SCALES FOR STAFFS OF COMMUNITY HOMES (CONTINUED)

RANGES

(Scales of 5 points to be selected from within each range)
(Subject to conditions of N.J.C. Circular No. N.O. 279)

Note: All rates given below are in English pounds. One English pound is equivalent to two U.S. dollars.

RANGE 6	RANGE 6A	RANGE 7	RANGE 7A
3096	3186	3474	3588
3186	3282	3588	3702
3282	3366	3702	3825
3366	3474	3825	3957
3474	3588	3957	4095
3588	3702	4095	4239
3702	3825	4239	4395
3825	3957	*4395	4545
3957	4095	4545	4689
4095	4239	4689	4842
4239	4395	4842	4992

RANGE 8	RANGE 8A	RANGE 9	RANGE 9A
4025	4239	4395	4545
4239	4395	4545	4689
4395	4545	4689	4842
4545	4689	4842	4992
4689	4842	4992	5103
4842	4992	5103	5250
4992	5103	5250	5406
5103	5250	5406	5577
		5577	5721

*Maximum salary point for Officers in charge of Group 2 homes (30-49 places)

FINANCE DEPARTMENT

NJC (MANUAL WORKERS) RATES OF PAY EFFECTIVE 31ST OCTOBER, 1977

Group	Hourly rate	Weekly rate	Including 65p service supplement after 5 years		Rates of pay Codes H1-H5
			Hourly rate	Weekly rate	
A	1.0586	39.70	1.0760	40.35	
B D/A	1.0693	40.10	1.0866	40.75	
C	1.0826	40.60	1.1000	41.25	
D	1.1200	42.00	1.1373	42.65	
E	1.1493	43.10	1.1666	43.75	E100 St. Paneras Wkshop
F	1.1813	44.30	1.1986	44.95	London Weighting 6 per week
G	1.2146	45.55	1.2320	46.20	= 20.1600 per hour
Semi-skilled I	1.1893	44.60	1.2066	45.25	
Semi-skilled II	1.1266	42.25	1.1440	42.90	
Driver/Attendant	1.1880	44.55	1.2053	45.20	
Catering helper	1.0538	39.52	1.0712	40.17	
Assistant cook	1.1045	41.42	1.1218	42.07	
Cook	1.1658	43.72	1.1832	44.37	
Home help	1.1266	42.25	1.1440	42.90	
Senior home help	1.1800	44.25	1.1973	44.90	Being Home help rate plus 2 per week
Care assistant CLI	1.1266	42.25	1.1440	42.90	
Care assistant CLII	1.1573	43.40	1.1746	44.05	
Senior care assistant	1.1666	43.75	1.1840	44.40	Being Care assistant CLI plus 1.50 per week

London weighting   4.37 per week paid as hourly permanent plus rate = 0.1165 per hour.
London excess   0.45 per week paid as hourly permanent plus rate = 0.0121 per hour.
Lead-in bonus   1.50 per week paid as hourly permanent plus rate = 0.0400 per hour.
Nation award   5.00 per week paid as hourly permanent plus rate = 0.1333 per hour.
  supplement

Shift pay (alternating) = 0.0850 per hour
Shift pay (rotating)   = 0.1360 per hour

Note: All rates given above are in English pounds. One English pound is equivalent to
       two U.S. dollars.

DOMESTIC HELP

In addition to the junior and senior staff at Oxford and
Cambridge, there is a category of in-house personnel referred
to as "domestic help". At Oxford these include the cook (Jane),
the cleaning woman (Linda), and the night staff (Ella and Helen,
one of whom assists the regular CCOs on the two-person evening
shift, and is paid by the hour). See preceding pages for
domestic help pay scale.

In addition to the domestic staff, there is the driver (Bob) who
is shared by both houses. His duties are to chauffeur the
children, staff, and sometimes parents and sundry others to
their various house-related functions. Bob's job is neither
"staff" nor "domestic", but a separate occupational ranking
within the Social Services. Finally, there are occasional
volunteers who take the children on local outings. During the
period of my study, Laura, a very pleasant and caring woman,
was involved in this way.

Who these people are, how they acquired their jobs, and something of their background will be dealt with in the illustrative
case histories that follow. What they do on the job and the
importance of their formal and informal roles within the
facility will be dealt with more extensively in various other
contexts throughout the book.

I will not attempt here to give detailed case histories for all
of the staff at the Center. Rather, I will offer a sampling of
new and established junior and senior staff, and show that,
notwithstanding the differences in their prior backgrounds or
work experiences, that nearly all members of staff became
residential childcare officers: (1) by accident, (2) had little
or had no prior work experience and/or formal training in this
role, (3) began as volunteers, (4) accepted the job in the
search for more meaningful work, (5) did so in many cases by
giving up less meaningful but more lucrative positions, (6) are
basically anti-intellectual in their approach to childcare,
(7) are currently disenchanted with their work, and suffer
collectively from a bad case of "anomie".

CASE HISTORIES

Oxford Staff

Cynthia:

We will begin this sampling of case histories with Cynthia, a newcomer to the field of childcare. Cynthia was raised in Africa and came to England 6 years ago to do postgraduate work in teaching. As a school teacher, she had a better paying position in Africa than the one she now has in childcare. However, at this point she had second thoughts about continuing her teaching career, and instead "just messed around" during her first 3 years in England. When she felt more at home in the country, she began to search for more meaningful and permanent work, work with people, work that would "offer me the kind of challenge I need to keep myself awake through life". How did she come by her job at Oxford?

> "And this particular one (job) was a pure accident, cause I went along to Town Hall to see if they had any vacancies ... preferably with children. So they sent me an application, which I sent back and they sent me an interview time and I came down here (to Oxford) for an interview, and that's that. And when I came to the interview, I didn't know what kind of job I was coming to in fact. So I just let fate or destiny bring me here."

Most childcare officers, in addition to the fortuitous way in which they arrived at the Center, were anti-intellectual in their approach to childcare. In fact, all but two of the child-care workers at the Center (the acting superintendent and new superintendent included) fit this characterization. On the job experience and one's own childhood background (if it was similar in its circumstances to the children they saw) was everything, while books and academic training came to little or nothing. Nor was this solely a function of the fact that most childcare workers had little formal education themselves. For example, even those few who had advanced formal academic training and/or social work degrees were often ambivalent about accepting the interpretations given by the psychiatric consultants regarding the nature of the child's problems and what to do about them. Most operated on folk understandings, "play it by ear" and "it's good if it works" recipes. These differing "vocabulary of motives" held by the consultants and staff often lead to many covert differences of opinion. Ironically, these contrary assessments by the staff ran concurrent with the high esteem CCOs had for consultants.

The author, as someone "studying" the "agency" as opposed to
"working in the agency", also fell prey to these early negative
assessments. This was partially but not entirely negated by my
involvement in house affairs and some of the staff's informal
off-the-job social life. However, the notion that "those who
can do, those who can't teach" died hard in this setting. From
my field notes of 21 January, 1978:

>"Shawn had worked in the insurance business a few years ago
>before taking his current job as 'residential childcare
>officer'. As he put it, 'It's quite a mouthful and a title
>no one uses around here. It doesn't mean very much anyway.'
>Shawn was talking of the importance of experience versus
>University training or advanced social work credentials.
>Cynthia had also taken this line that 'dealing with people
>was different than looking at people' and that in dealing
>with them, you got to know them in ways that looking at
>them or reading about them in books could not duplicate."

All of the above, which is actually a small synopsis of a long
conversation I had separately with Cynthia and Shawn during my
first days at Oxford, were directed at me and contained a touch
of irony tempered with a good humored contempt for sociology.
However, I have heard similar attacks against the consultants
and other social service higher echelon personnel who were "out
of touch" with the everyday workings of the house. This "out-
of-touchness resulted not only from their lack of direct involvement with the children, but was compounded by their formal
social work education, and their different childhood and family
background. While the CCOs were pleased with their involvement
in the family therapy aspect of the assessment process (a facet
of the work that made it more than "making tea and wiping bums")
many felt that viewing the "family dynamics" as primarily or
solely the source of the child's problems was often "a lot of
bullshit"; and that poverty, unemployment, and the lack of
opportunity offered a better explanation of the family's
troubles.

Finally there was the problem of staff morale. This was seen
to be at an all-time low during the "transition period", i.e.,
the time preceding the move to Queen's Road. Everyone viewed
themselves and others as being in a "holding pattern" or just
"marking time" during this stage of the agency's development.
For the past couple of years, workers have, by their own admission, had little enthusiasm for their work. There were many
reasons for this, e.g., staff was waiting to see who the new
superintendent would be and what his policies would be like;

while the move to Queen's Road was generally disliked, it was
an unknown and everyone wondered how it would be with two houses
under one roof, in the move some staff would get promotions and
pay raises, others in the competition would not (this in turn
promoted anxieties and antagonism among the staff); many new
persons and others with seniority had through experience come
to question the wisdom of reception and assessment centers in
general; and finally, there was much concern over what many staff
saw as the possible demise of family therapy with the move to
Queen's Road.

Judy:

If Cynthia was a newcomer to Oxford, Judy had been there since
its inception. She is one of the few workers to have had a prior
background, if not with reception and assessment centers, then
at least with children in a "long care stay facility". Like
many of the other CCOs, Judy began her work with children as a
volunteer. In fact, she volunteered for 18 months with what
was then the National Children's Home. That was about 10 years
ago. Like the other senior CCOs, she came up through the ranks
to her present position as "teamleader" or "head of home". The
National Children's Home ran its own course of study, and as a
result of her experience there, she acquired a "home office
certificate". She then left that position for a job at a
"reception and assessment center" in one of the other boroughs
in London, where she worked for about 3 years, and from there
to her current position at Oxford. The three years at the last
center she characterizes this way:

> "Well, I say reception and assessment center, certainly
> looking at it now I wouldn't classify it as reception and
> assessment. But that's what it was classed as"(by the
> department of social services).

In short, her prior training, while it gave her experience in
working with children, was not the sort of work experience that
was required of her at Oxford. In this sense, even Judy, who
had perhaps the most in the way of prior work experience, was
not really trained for the sort of work she was required to do
upon first arriving at Oxford. As for her search for more
meaningful work, she tells us about her work at the National
Children's Home.

"I just wouldn't like to compare them (the job situation
then versus current working conditions). There was no such
thing as a 40 hour working week. We were paid a salary and
you worked, if necessary, a 24 hour day, 7 days a week. It
was no such thing as two days off a week plus time off every
day. If you were lucky, you got a day and a half off every
week. If you weren't lucky, you mightn't get any."

And, of course, there was no family therapy in either of those
programs. This was something Judy and the other childcare
officers considered a very big "perk" or on-the-job benefit.
Regarding the role of family therapy within the Center (an
unusual feature even now in England) Judy says:

"And it makes you really think what you're doing . And I
think the other thing is it makes you look very seriously
around you at the other establishments (for childcare) and
you realize that you've got something that's precious."

If Judy came to Oxford like most other workers, in search of
more meaningful work, what did she find?

"I think basically I've been very happy here; I wouldn't
have stayed 6 years if I hadn't been."

Her general contentment with her position at Oxford over the
long run stems in part from the fact that she gets along fairly
well with Sylvia and is herself a "senior staff". In fact,
there may be more than a casual connection between the former
and latter. We have already indicated that those who do not get
along with the acting superintendent do not seem to get along
in their careers.

However, Judy's longstanding positive assessment of her job
tends to conceal her current feelings.

  JJ: "What's it like working here now?"
  Judy: "At the moment I've got the most mixed feelings in
         the world, but I think it's all the upheaval (the
         transition period) of knowing that we're not staying
         here and that something else (Queen's Road) is around
         the corner. There are times at the moment when I'd
         just like to go and throw it all up in the air and
         just run away for 6 months."

Apart from the anxiety of the move and all the imponderables it
presented, there were other sources of discontent.

> "It's frustrating sometimes because you're supposed to be
> on paper — head of house. But, in fact, you don't have
> ultimate responsibility (Sylvia does). And yet, if anything
> goes wrong you might very well be held accountable. So you
> have feelings about that ... when things go wrong, you're
> responsible; but while they're going right, somebody else
> (the acting superintendent) likes to take the credit."

Like Cynthia and many others, Judy also had "communication
problems" with her immediate superior. This was so notwithstanding their longtime friendship and feelings of mutual
respect. In fact, Judy and Sylvia had much in common, e.g.,
both were loud, open, brash and earthy in a way none of the
other workers could match.

> "But I do find it difficult to talk about some of the things
> with her (Sylvia) that I would like to be able to, in a
> different sort of way, rather than feeling that things go
> on behind your back. In fact, you know they do, because
> there's a grapevine wherever you are."

Digby:

As a final case study at Oxford, consider Digby, the new
superintendent, who displaced Sylvia toward the end of the
study. Digby, while he had a longstanding acquaintance with
social services as an administrator, had not had any direct
experience either as an administrator or worker in a children's
reception and assessment center. Notwithstanding all this, he
was about to become the head of what was probably the largest,
most modern and costly facility of this type in London, perhaps
in all of England. How did this happen? Well, it happened in
much the same way many of the other staff came to Oxford, by
accident.

> Digby: "Well, I felt that after 5 or 6 years (at his last
> job in Northern England as a 'field social worker')
> it was becoming a matter of working the rest of my
> life until you retire here, or you would have to
> think in terms of if you wanted a new experience to
> widen your horizons. So initially, I contacted
> (the borough the center was in) about a fieldwork
> job similar to the one I'd been doing... I was
> invited down for an interview out of the blue, and

out of the course of that, Queen's Road came into
things; and I was asked whether I may be interested
in eventually moving in that direction (to become
the superintendent of the new residential facility)
as opposed to field work again.... Certainly at
that stage, although I had an interest in residential
social work, I couldn't have felt that I had the
experience or the qualifications to assume responsibility as head of an observation and assessment
center."

Without assessing Digby's competence to assume the position of
superintendent (he may in fact do a good job) there is the prior
question of how someone with his obvious lack of formal credentials acquired the job in the first place. After all, Social
Services had 3 years in which to conduct a search for just the
right person. This set of circumstances was, I believe, as much
a surprise and mystery to Digby as anyone. Indeed, one had the
impression that Digby had not so much won the position in an
open competition with others based upon his superior qualifications (as we expect in civil service contests) but rather that
there were no other takers (apart from the acting superintendent
for the past 3 years who was an acknowledged applicant for the
job). This situation did not, I believe, result from a conspiracy in the "old boy" mode, i.e., some higher echelon person or
persons in Social Services did not hire an old friend for the
job. The job was advertised in appropriate places and all
comers were given serious consideration. The problem seems to
have been that Social Services needed a new superintendent for
the facility quickly; and apart from Digby and Sylvia, there
were, for whatever reason, no takers. As a result, Digby did
not so much have to convince the local authority to bestow the
position upon him as Social Services had to convince Digby to
accept it.

Once again we see that staff typically came by the job by
accident and had no real special prior formal training or
qualifications for the job. We see too from the above excerpt
that Digby took this job in an effort to "broaden his horizons".
This meant not only going a step higher on the career ladder,
but moving, as many sought to do, from probation into Social
Services with the national "reorganization" of 1971. There
were many reasons for this. Some understanding in this case
of the push part of the push-pull factor of job selection can
be had from the following excerpt from the transcribed interviews.

"But a lot of people were at that stage (at the time of the
reorganization) concerned about the direction in which we
were going. They were a little bit anxious about who became
very penal minded, (about probation becoming) a penal
oriented organization. There was some concern about losing
our work with the juvenile people because it was envisaged,
and still is, (that) eventually social services would take
total responsibility for all juvenile offenders up until the
age of 18. (At the time of the study, that had not come
about.) ... And there was quite a bit of movement at the
time of reorganization from probation to social services."

Here we see a number of things motivating Digby, not just the
acceptance of the higher status and more lucrative position
that dropped in his lap "out of the blue". There was also an
effort on his part to be involved in what he understood to be a
politically and morally more meaningful form of work. His
political liberalism can be gleaned from the following passages.

Digby: "And I think ... social work itself and social
            workers are very establishment people; and because
            of our links with the local authority and the
            agency, are not exerting the sort of influences
            that could really have a meaningful impact on the
            people they're working with. I don't think we do
            anything for a family to remove four or five
            children. I think that what we could be doing is
            saying to the politicians, look, if you provide
            this family with another 30 pounds a week, that
            would mean something. Going in and removing the
            kids, that means nothing, and is costing a lot
            more.... And these are professional (social work)
            organizations and (they) are good example, I think,
            of preserving the status quo.... I often wonder to
            myself if we are the conscience of the society or
            whether we are society's conscience, and I'd much
            rather agree with the first, but I've got a hell of
            a feeling we're the second."

This excerpt, I think, expressed the feelings of most of the
Center's staff. What is ironic is that at the time of Digby's
arrival (this interview was soon after) I doubt that anyone
believed him capable of such sentiments. He was type cast after
his first formal in-house meeting as a "stiff organization man",
something that made many on both the junior and senior staff
uneasy. Apart from the political liberalism in the above

excerpt, there is an implicit anti-intellectualism in his dis-
trust and dismay of professional social work organizations. He
was not, after all, a university credentialed social worker, but
had come up through the ranks. This should have endeared him
to most of the staff. If it did not, it was because the ranks
he came up through were different than their own, i.e., they
rose through Social Service and he through probation. The
latter was viewed with suspicion as being overly structured and
domineering. In fact, a kind of Brendan Behan "Borstal Boy"
image of Digby pervaded the Center upon his arrival.[1]*

Apart from his opinions about social work and why he accepted
the job in the first place, how did the Center's new superintendent feel about his new role. We have already noted his initial
anxiety. This anxiety was mitigated somewhat by his orientation
toward the job, i.e., had he intended it to become his life's
work, he might well have felt even greater anxiety than one
normally encounters upon accepting a new job and higher position
of authority. As it happens, he was not oriented in this way.

> "I think that as with anybody who sort of takes on a new
> field of work (as he was doing) one is wondering about
> progress and evaluation and so on. The things that I have
> second thoughts about have been very practical issues
> concerned with me, and not necessarily issues related to
> the job or the type of work that I'm having a go at now.
> I still see it as an unusual opportunity for someone in my
> situation. I think that I'm setting myself time limits
> which in a sense, may be a bit of an escape (clause) for me.
> At this time, I'm not thinking in terms of 10 or 15 years
> at Queen's Road. I'm thinking more in short term, and
> seeing how things work out.... Perhaps if I did (think in
> terms of long-term career commitments) I would worry more
> about how things are going."

How is such an orientation on Digby's part likely to affect the
running of the agency? Basically there are two positions in
the formal organizational literature that relate to this
question. One is the need for organization stability through
a continuity in command. The second, and inherently antagonistic position, is the need for "new blood" and innovation to
insure against organizational stagnation.[2] One way to get the
latter, at the expense of the former, is to have people join

---

*Superscript numbers refer to Notes at end of book.

the agency who are not committed to long-term stays and feel
no overwhelming need for career advancement within the organization. Given the nature of civil service (indeed most organizational arrangements) the opposite sort of leadership would
insure a built-in conservatism to change, stemming from one's
vested interests in "not making waves" and getting ahead. In
this regard, Digby, and a number of other new junior staff,
provided "new blood" and the prospect of change. The question
arises, where was the agency in terms of this process of too
much versus too little change? I believe the overwhelming
consensus would have been that the Center had been subject to
too little change for too long. The question in the minds of
most staff was not whether a change was needed, but rather the
nature of the change, and what it would bring — would things
change for the better or worse? At the time that Digby assumed
the helm, the answer to this question (indeed Digby himself)
was a complete unknown. Unknowns, while they allow for hope,
also generate a good deal of anxiety. Such was the state of the
Oxford junior and senior staff at the time of the new superintendent's arrival and the impending move to the new facility.

Cambridge Staff

We have discussed what some of the staff at Oxford were like.
In what ways, if any, were they different from the CCOs at
Cambridge? For one thing, there was at Cambridge, particularly
among the new junior staff, a disproportionate number of "new
blood" types. By this, you will remember I mean a basically
humanistic sort of individual who is employed as a childcare
officer, who is usually younger and better educated. And yet,
one who comes to the job with no long-term commitment to it,
or any consuming desire of going up through the ranks. While
one's commitment to an intellectual approach to childcare
varied considerably within this group, "new bloods", whether
guided by prior experience and common sense, or formal training
were characteristically more open and outspoken in their views
in staff meetings and generally more interested in major shifts
in agency policy and goals.

Philip:

At the time of our interview, Philip worked at Cambridge for
5 months, and is a prime example of this new, younger and
better educated temporary help (their intentions to be temporary
may be known or unknown to management). He had completed 2
years of a 4-year university education, and felt at that

juncture that he needed to take a break from his studies in
order to earn some money, after which time he hoped to return
to school to finish his education. Following a series of
temporary odd jobs, he found himself in London looking for more
meaningful work. While perusing a social work magazine, he saw
an ad for a job working with children with speech impediments.
Given that his prior training had to do in part with linguistics,
he felt that he might combine this interest with more meaningful work. In fact, earlier (in the interview) he told the
author of his efforts to "imagine London as a big campus". His
application for the job was in keeping with this orientation.
However, instead of this job he was offered a position at
Oxford. Here again, Philip views his entry into the field of
childcare as sheer accident.

> "Eventually I was offered this job, and when it came, I had
> not been thinking of doing work like this at all.... I had
> wanted to find a job where I could do something well and
> be appreciated for it. I imagined it was this ... ha ha
> (ironic laughter)."

Since the administrative offices of the Center were at Oxford,
Philip went there for his initial interviews. He also spent
the day there to "have a look see". Here is his initial
impression:

> "The whole atmosphere reminded me in a lot of ways, when
> it came down to the basics, like the smell of mental
> hospitals that I'd worked in before on vacations. And
> there was just something dead about it in the sense that ...
> what I used to hate about mental hospitals is the way that
> the staff used to form a thick skin — they hardened
> terribly. And what they do is treat the patients very much
> like plants. You water them, and you grow rows of wheel-
> chairs and things. And when I came up here first thing the
> smell put me off.... It wasn't the regimentation, but it
> was a kind of over control that I didn't like."[3]

Not only did Philip not look forward to the prospect of working
at Oxford, but he told them so. As a result, he received a
position at Cambridge, since there was an opening there as well.

> "I suppose in a sense it means I prefer to work at Cambridge
> than Oxford, and I feel that I can work better and express
> myself better in a looser environment."

Philip sought to work with disadvantaged children because he
felt that such work would be meaningful to him. The same was
true of most of the other CCOs. The question arises, why was
work with disadvantaged children so universally meaningful to
the staff? The answer, in part, has to do with the fact that
most of the staff were also disadvantaged as children. Philip,
however, was not. He too wanted to help disadvantaged children,
but less from empathetic compassion, than from compassion
coupled with guilt.

> "I wanted, I suppose like most people who have taken a
> social science degree, you feel a sense, well people of my
> background (middle class) I suppose, feel a sense of guilt
> in a way. It's not a dramatic thing, but you want to do
> something useful. You want to put something back immedi-
> ately (into society) before you do anything else. And
> that's why I did it (went for a job interview at Oxford)."

The fact is that many of the CCOs from working class backgrounds
at the Center, with or without a formal social science education,
felt as Philip did. However, the source of their motivation
was different, as was their orientation to the work. Philip
was probably more introspective and intellectual in his approach
than most. However, he too felt that the prior background of
the worker was an essential ingredient in the worker's ability
to empathize with the child, or at least to be able to do so
quickly, inasmuch as many of the children were not at the Center
for long periods of time. Regarding the length of time taken
to complete an evaluation, Philip felt (as many others did)
that the children were often held longer than need be.

> "And I know that there is quite a big turnover in staff or
> has been; and I can see why. I think people come in ambiti-
> ous, and they're told that there is valuable work going on;
> but somehow this seems to get blocked.... One can only
> assume that the kids are getting blocked here and staying
> much too long because nobody is finding them places outside.
> They shouldn't be here too long."

In reference to one's ability to empathize with the children
with respect to one's own background, he tells us:

> "I think that an assessment of certain kinds of kids can be
> done in two minutes, and is done by the more experienced
> staff, and particularly those having a common background.
> And to name them, I'd say ... Alec is like that, he knows
> their backgrounds, and also May (the night staff) and Bob

(the van driver). I find that one session (staff meeting
used to discuss the children) is essential cause I don't see
that I am ever from my background and everything, going to
get essentially that close to them (the children). I am a
visitor from outer space who is staying for a while. And
my case is a bit more extreme than the others (workers)
because I know that I am only going to stay for a year."

While Philip has only been on the unit for 5 months, he is
already disenchanted with the work. Inasmuch as he is able to
treat the job as part of his continuing education, he feels that
he is benefiting from the experience; but he is not convinced
that many of the children are. The notion that the Center is
actually more therapeutic for the staff than for the children
was a contention supported by two of the three outside consultants who felt they spent more time dealing with the staff's
personal and inter-personal problems than the children's.
Having attended many of the staff meetings, I believe that they
were not overstating the case.

Philip put it this way:

"I'm optimistic in terms of what it (the job) has done to
me and (my) personal development. But it does worry me
because I think that one can come into a job like this and
if it is continuing to have children like this, the sort of
person who tends to come into this work not selflessly let's
say, doesn't really meet his or her problems, but they are
suspended. What they find is one big supportive environment
for themselves I think.... When you're getting things
solved with certain kinds of kids, I think the energy tends
to get turned toward the staff; and I don't think that is
very healthy."

Another source of disenchantment, especially among the new staff,
stemmed from the fact that they were not really involved in any
meaningful way in the assessment process, and not at all in
family therapy.

Phillip: "It (the Center) is one big holding operation.
And because you were there, in a sort of holding
operation, it is sometimes difficult to feel that
the work we are doing was getting anywhere. I
didn't see much of the assessment because of the
normal vagaries of the rota system (the way in
which staff work shifts were scheduled) and

communications within Cambridge, didn't really make me feel
that I was assessing anybody. Nobody asked for the information (he had) at all. Nobody that is outside of Cambridge
(the assessments, remember, took place in Oxford in staff
meetings)."

In fact, many of the new staff who had been with the Center for
as long as 6 months had not yet had a case of their own, i.e.,
been directly involved in any aspect of family therapy. This
led many new workers to feel betrayed in that they looked
forward to such an involvement and were told that it was to be
an integral part of their job at the time of the interview.
Indeed, many felt that they were receiving no formal on-the-job
training. All of this and more contributed to the hard feelings
junior staff held toward senior staff and toward London Social
Services in general.

Such were some of the sentiments and circumstances of the junior
staff at Cambridge. Let us now look at a member of the senior
staff and how he assessed his own work and the work of others.
A look at formal organization chart number 2 shows that Ann is
the current "teamleader" at Cambridge under the staff reorganization plan enacted prior to the move to the new assessment center.
However, Alec had held this position for the last 5 years; and
is really the one that the old Cambridge staff relates to as
their "head of home". Ann as a newcomer to that position, is
viewed as a complete unknown to the Cambridge staff, at least
with respect to how her administration will affect the old
order at Cambridge. With this in mind, I will use Alec as an
example of senior staff at Cambridge, since it was under his
direction that the unit came to take the form it did.

Alec:

We will begin this case history, as we have the others, with a
consideration of how Alec first became acquainted with childcare and how and why he came to be employed in his current
capacity at the Center.

Alec first took a job on a volunteer basis (as did nearly all
CCOs at this Center) about 9 years ago working with severely
disturbed children, most of whom were later institutionalized.
He worked at this position for 2 years, during which time he
maintained a regular full-time job in "cost accounting".
Following this, he became involved in running various social
clubs in socially deprived areas (five nights a week) on a
voluntary basis. There, through a friend of his, he met people

in the childcare network; and because he "prefers people to
books and figures", he looked for some way to become involved
with people as a career. Alec came from a working class family
and neighborhood, and because of this, wanted to help people
with similar backgrounds. In answer to the question "how did
you first get into the field of childcare?" he tells us:

> "Well, because I suppose it's got something to do with my
> upbringing. I was brought up in what one would describe as
> a fairly rundown area of London that had a fair amount of
> delinquency. And I was always interested, that's why I
> helped on a volunteer basis; and felt that I had a lot of
> skill, firstly in empathizing with some of the kids that we
> were trying to help. I found it very easy in actual fact
> to put myself into their position, not necessarily agreeing
> with what they did, but that I could imagine, I knew the
> pressures. A lot of my friends ended up in what could be
> termed as custodial sorts of places for various amounts of
> time because they were in trouble."

Alec took a part-time course at the University (two nights a
week) and having completed the program, came to London to be
married. At that point, he took a "professional training
course" for a 13-month period and received what is known as a
"residential certificate of care with young people". This
entailed readings in psychology and psychiatry, a good deal of
written work and field placements for practical experience.
This degree is not equivalent to a M.S.W. (Masters of Social
Work) in the United States. The English equivalent is called
C.Q.S.W. (Certificate of Qualification in Social Work), and only
one childcare officer, including the senior staff, held that
degree. With this certificate, Alec acquired a job at another
London childcare facility as a "deputy", a position one under
"teamleader". However, the second week on the job the person
in charge had a nervous breakdown (the superintendent in charge
at Oxford and Cambridge, before Sylvia, also had a nervous
breakdown) and Alec found himself in charge of the unit. His
new position required that he live at the residence, and after
4 months, he found this intolerable and quit. This was followed
by a 3-month "look around", i.e., a search for another job.
During that time he cleaned windows and reflected upon whether
or not to continue in the field of childcare. Toward the end
of this period he applied for an advertised position at Cambridge,
and after a 3-month wait, acquired the job as "head of unit" or
"teamleader".

To sum up, Alec seems to be an exception to the rule. He did have prior experience in childcare, he did apply for the job at Cambridge, and he did know (more or less) what that job entailed. However, during his three - month stint at window washing and the second thoughts he had about childcare, had the job at Cambridge not materialized, there was the real possibility of Alec becoming a childcare worker dropout. If there was some variation on this point, then Alec ran true to form on many others. He came from a working class background, wanted to help others in similar circumstances, left a more lucrative job as cost accountant to do so, began as a volunteer, and put a lot more faith in his practical experience and personal background as a guide to childcare than in formal education, training, or the expert opinions of outside second parties.

Although Alec has been at Cambridge for about 5 years, we will not consider until the following chapter the "before and after" of his administration. Rather, in keeping with our format, we will present only his current assessment of his work and his place in the hierarchy. In particular, we will be concerned with how Alec viewed the Center and his role in it, during the "transition period".

One current and persistent problem according to Alec, was Cambridge's "step-child" status. While "being down the road" and not at Oxford "gave us a bit more freedom", it also

> "... opened us up for more abuse if you like. You know, if
> you want to blame something (on someone) you look to resi-
> dential management. Well, I think Cambridge has been used
> like that. If things are going wrong, or something is not
> quite right, or people are not feeling right about things,
> then it's easy if you got somewhere down the road that you
> can just say, all right, that's where the problem is."

In addition to the "step-child" problem, Alec did not get along well with Meg, his deputy (see formal organization chart number 1). Part of this resentment on Meg's part stemmed from the fact that she was at Oxford 3 months before Alec arrived, and, as deputy, felt that she was next in line for the position as head-of-home. While Alec claims that Meg had not formally applied for the job, she was nevertheless resentful that it was Alec and not her who got it.

Alec: "Meg and I, for some reason, never hit it off. You
        know, over 5 years we obviously evolved a system, we
        both stayed there, where we could work together
        reasonably well; but I would never say that I was
        comfortable with Meg as my deputy."

Apart from problems with his second in command, Alec notes that
he did not get along well with Sylvia (the acting superintendent) and that things were only marginally better during the
former superintendent's administration.

"I found that as far as the hierarchy was concerned, and
specifically Sylvia, I have a lot of problems."

If Sylvia and Alec did not get along well, neither did Sylvia
and Meg. In fact, there were many on the staff who were
antagonistic toward Sylvia, and to whom she returned the
sentiment.

Alec's most current concern is where he will fit in the new
order of things when the move to Queen's Road is finally
completed. Such anxieties and ambiquities you will remember
were longstanding. The move was pending for the past 2 years,
and was constantly being rescheduled due to construction delays.

Alec: "That's where my difficulties are lying at the
        moment, because you know the job description for my
        new job (in the new facility) is nonexistent. At
        the moment, I'm finding it very difficult to find a
        way in here (Oxford, where Alec was temporarily
        assigned when Ann took over as new teamleader at
        Cambridge).
JJ: "You're sort of hanging out for awhile."
Alec: "Yeah, hanging out is the right word, and it's a
        very uncomfortable position."

Alec's worries have become more focused of late, and he is now
concerned that he does not end up "domestic bursar" or "matron",
i.e., a person in charge of food and clothing orders and the
organization of the domestic's work shifts. As things stand
Alec will be third in command at the new facility, and "matron"
is the traditional role for the third in command. In fact,
there is now above the door to Alec's office in the new facility
a sign that says "MATRON".

Alec's anxiety about the move and his new role was shared by
most staff. Not only were they concerned that Alec hold a
position as a mediator and buffer zone between Digby and Sylvia
and the junior staff; but they were worried as well about their
own jobs in the new setting. In fact, everyone awaited the
move, some with hope and all with trepidation.

Mary:

If Philip has only been at Cambridge for a few months, and
Alec since shortly after its opening, Mary has been with the
unit for about a year and a half. True to form, she began as a
volunteer (for 5 months at Oxford), sought more meaningful
employment, had no prior work experience in childcare, was
basically anti-intellectual in her approach, and was currently
disenchanted with the work, partly at least, because of the
effects of the "transition period".

> *JJ:*   "How did you get into childcare?"
> *Mary:* "There's a set-up in this country called Community
>   Service Volunteers. When you actually apply to
>   Community Service Volunteers, which is what I did,
>   they sent me to Oxford, and I worked in a capacity
>   as staff. I mean, I had all the duties that a staff
>   can have, but didn't get paid for it, or I got
>   six pounds a week for it, which just about covered
>   my bus fare."
> *JJ:*   "How did you get to Cambridge?"
> *Mary:* "A vacancy occurred; one of the staff left, and I
>   applied for it, and got it."
> *JJ:*   "How did you end up wanting to volunteer in the first
>   place?"
> *Mary:* "My training was secretarial. I was a secretary for
>   quite a long time, and the last job I had before
>   coming into this work was an interviewer in an
>   employment agency finding people jobs, and I really
>   enjoyed that. I mean you had to have office back-
>   ground, which I had, and I really enjoyed meeting
>   people and trying to help them with a pretty basic
>   problem, which was to find suitable employment.
>   But, the big but, was the pressure on me. You know,
>   we had a target (for placing a certain number of
>   people every month) because the agency charged the
>   potential employer 10% of the salary (of the person
>   they hired) and we got 1%, which was added to our
>   basic wage.... The pressure was on to push them
>   into any old job. Time was their (the employment

agency's) thing. I would have preferred to do it at
my own pace; but you know altruism is out in that
kind of agency. So you were there to place people
as quickly as possible. It led to a lot of dishonesty
and exploitive practices.... You know I thought I
had to get out. (Mary had the job for 8 months.)
So, I mean I realized by that time what I didn't like,
and I thought, well, there is only one thing for it,
I'm not going back being a secretary again. I'm
going to try social work."

Ironically, it was her experience in the employment agency that
first inspired her to want to work with people in a helping way.
Inasmuch as that agency didn't allow for it, and she had a
husband who worked with disturbed boys in an assessment center
(another one), she decided to try that. She entered the field
of childcare as many of the other workers did, by first volun-
teering in order to gain some experience and *entrée* to the
childcare network.

As for the current state of affairs, Mary also felt anxious
about the move to the new facility, anxious to see how the new
superintendent would affect the agency's past policies, and
anxious about the nature of work within the "institutional
setting" that she felt awaited them all at Queen's Road. However, Mary was an exception in this regard. She did not hold
the notion that one's job satisfaction necessarily expanded
directly with one's responsibility and the expanding democrati-
zation of the agency. She was not at all sure that she wanted
all that responsibility or that much democracy. That's not to
say she would have preferred working at Oxford (where she
started as a volunteer). In fact, we are told in the course of
the interview that she gets along fine with Alec, and not at
all well with Sylvia. Still, she feels some uneasiness with
all of Marilyn's (the current deputy) efforts to run in-house
self assessment groups and minimize in-house formal structure.

"Marilyn, from what I've seen, is taking her responsibility
very seriously. I mean (she) is very much for a democratic
way of doing things.... I mean she was talking on Wednesday
about peer group assessment ... and seems to want some sort
of forum where we will discuss each other's weaknesses....
The impression I get is that Marilyn doesn't want to
differentiate between the fact that she is a grade 4 and
I'm a grade 2, and Philip is a grade 1. She doesn't want
to acknowledge that too much. We're all counted the same.
And I'm not too sure if I go along with that or not. I
would get apprehensive about it."

Why was Mary concerned about this issue? Briefly, she felt
that one's income and status should be commensurate with one's
responsibility. Her concern was that she would get more
responsibility than she is paid for or than her rank infers;
while Marilyn might find in all this democracy a way to relin-
quish some of the responsibility that is rightfully hers.
While in no way inferring that the deputy had in fact not lived
up to the requirements of her office (indeed she seemed a
conscientious worker) the author can only concur with the politically astute Mary, that such a possibility existed. Mary was
reluctant to partake fully in a policy of total openness on
other grounds as well. During the transition period, preceding
the move to the new facility, some childcare officers went from
Cambridge to Oxford and some from Oxford to Cambridge. While
there was generally a lot of basic trust among the old established staff at Cambridge headed by Alec, there was with the
reorganization many unknowns introduced into each house. This
new circumstance did little to perpetuate a feeling of basic
trust.

> *Mary:*   "I'm not too keen on peer group assessments for a
>   lot of reasons. I don't know if I want to discuss
>   my weaknesses with all members of staff. Some I
>   would, some not. It involves a lot of trust, and
>   we're in such a state of flux at the moment, (Ann
>   is the new and unknown teamleader coming from Oxford,
>   the former opposition camp) and I want to know a bit
>   more about it" (before fully committing herself).

In short, a great many things have made Mary, and all of the
other childcare officers very cautious during this period. All
of this anxiety, notwithstanding its different or common origins,
has resulted in putting a damper on worker enthusiasm and led
to a distinct reduction in the level of childcare within the
Center.

In addition to the common denominators in the staff's backgrounds and current orientations, there was also a kind of
political schizophrenia operating among some childcare officers.
While nearly all came from working-class backgrounds themselves,
and considered themselves socialists, Marxists, strong labor
advocates, or at the very least, liberals and unionists, many
held what could be considered politically conservative positions
on a great many issues. For example, people on the S.S. (Social
Security) ought to "damn well get off the S.S.") or better yet,
the S.S. should be discontinued, inasmuch as unemployment

benefits and other subsidies only promoted a lack of industry.
People should, after a little help in hard times, "pull themselves up by their bootstraps". If they don't, they must be
lazy or "fiddling".

While the children at the Center were not living a life of
luxury, and staff sometimes complained of insufficient funds,
others expressed the position (to the author) that things were
too plush for the children's own good. After all if the main
goal of the agency was to reunite the child and his family,
giving the child a better home than his family could provide
would mitigate against this. If the child was "incorrigible",
the parent could more easily leave him in "care" with a good
conscience. If the parents or parent was upset at the loss of
the child to the agency, (however that happened in the first
place) then they might become at least ambivalent about the
child returning home if the agency provided what the parent saw
as a preferred environment, or at least an acceptable temporary
respite. Others felt that children in care, play the agency
off against the parents in much the same way that sought after
neutral or teetering nations play off "democratic" and
"totalitarian" states against each other for gain. In short,
some staff believed that the Center was too good to the children
for their own good.

In keeping with this contention, workers who generally felt that
things could have been much better for staff in terms of junior/
senior staff relationships and communication patterns, pay benefits, autonomy and openness within the agency, further involvement in family therapy, higher staff-to-children ratios, and
shorter work shifts (or fewer of them), never referred to problems or shortages as they related "to the best interest of the
child". One member of the staff put it this way.

"I think it's doing good for certain kinds of kids, (to be
a part of the Center) kids with highly disturbed families....
But when you got kids who are I suppose the more traditional
type, that I think in a sense tend to be hangers-on, and the
malingerers, then you got nothing to do with them here. In a
sense they become worse hangers-on and malingerers because
they are here. I don't really think that there is anything
we can do for them."

Some staff held the same view of the children's parents with
respect to their association with the agency.

3

A House Divided: Intra- and Inter-House Rivalries

There was between Oxford and Cambridge a strong feeling of
"them and us". Each of the houses had evolved their own form
of leadership, traditions, work habits, interpersonal relationships, political allegiances, and cohort of children. I will
begin this chapter with a consideration of "them and us" as it
relates to the two units, and then go on to treat these feelings
and their effects as they relate to junior and senior staff,
consultants and staff, children and staff, and finally parents
and staff.

OXFORD AND CAMBRIDGE

To begin to get some understanding of the differences between
Oxford and Cambridge one would do well to consider the temperaments of the house leaders, since both were very influential in
shaping the units in their own image. In fact, most of the
differences between the two houses are more often than not
formulated by staff in terms of the different temperaments of
the two long-term heads of home — Sylvia and Alec.

From the perspective of the Cambridge staff, Alec is more
democratic, delegates authority more often, is better at keeping
lines of communication open between junior and senior staff and
succeeds in this because he has succeeded in winning the trust
of staff, i.e., he does not hold grudges or engage in double
dealings, and has given the staff greater autonomy than they
had known when Sylvia was their head of home. While there were
things about the structure and intent of childcare that the
Cambridge staff did not like, very few of these were seen as
Alec's fault. Not only did they praise Alec's administration,
but they were hard critics of Sylvia's reign during the time
that she held Alec's position.

How did the Oxford staff assess Sylvia's performance as an
administrator? There was, among the staff, a wide range of
opinion on this matter. All felt that she was a caring, able,
and conscientious, childcare worker. Some felt that she got
"a raw deal" and should have been promoted from acting superintendent to superintendent. Many liked her informal and folky
way of running the house. What the staff did not like was the
lack of basic trust that pervaded Oxford. This it was felt
resulted from Sylvia and her past dealings with staff. Her
administration was characterized by her taking credit for other
people's good works when things went well, and shifting blame
from herself to innocent others when it did not. However, it
should be noted that it was generally conceded, both by her
friends and ardent critics, that such unpopular acts were more
a thing of the past than current practice. In short, the staff
felt that Sylvia had "mellowed out" to some extent. Whether
this positive change was the result of a different power
structure or her "mellowing", no one knew. While everyone was
glad with the change, whatever the cause, the past dies hard,
and many felt that prudence ought still to prevail as the better
part of valor. The net result was that staff were very cautious
in staff meetings about what they said and how they said it.
This, of course, subverted to a large extent the intent of staff
meetings to deal openly with personal or in-house problems.

Sylvia also held a tighter reign than Alec in delegating authority or in allowing as much autonomy in the work setting. All
in-house rules were seen as emanating from "Central Headquarters",
i.e., Sylvia's office. Notwithstanding all of this, Sylvia had,
at least among a sector of the staff, a strong loyalty and
following. As for how the staff at Oxford viewed Alec's efforts
at Cambridge, there was very little said one way or the other.
If Alec had few rooters at Oxford, he had few critics. A
partial reason for this, I feel, is that the two houses had a
great deal of autonomy (at least, at the time of the study),
and while Sylvia's influence was felt in both houses, Alec's
was primarily restricted to Cambridge. This resulted in
Cambridge staff knowing more about Sylvia than Oxford's staff
knew about Alec. Some indication of Alec's influence on
Cambridge can be had from his account of the circumstances he
inherited upon his arrival and how he managed to alter them
over time.

"I think the first thing was that the first year was pretty
difficult because I came into an establishment (Cambridge)
where most of the staff didn't take any responsibility, or
weren't given any responsibility for dealing with most of
the things that came up. To give you an example, there
seemed to be only one person actually answering the phone
and taking messages (as opposed to any member of staff who
happened to be available). When decisions were made, a
phone call was made out of the unit to someone up here (at
Oxford) to make the decision, usually Sylvia. And originally, before I got there, Sylvia actually ran the unit (at
Cambridge)."

In addition to gaining Cambridge greater autonomy from Oxford,
and giving the staff more autonomy, Alec had other in-house
problems as well.

"The first year I had great difficulty. There was quite a
bit of resentment from my deputy (Meg) when I got there,
who for some reason or another, although she didn't apply
for the job (as teamleader), couldn't see why she hadn't
got it. The first year was pretty difficult because groups
weren't used to dealing with stuff as it came up, but left
it or rang up somebody (at Oxford). Most of the staff were
pretty divided, and there weren't cohesive groups. And my
first priority was to give them enough confidence for them
to start acting in terms of a team, rather than as a very
tight, one person making decisions and the rest doing the
basic work. And I had battles galore to get that into
operation."

Apart from intra- and inter-house staff problems, there was
Alec's general outlook on childcare. This too was different
than Sylvia's. The relationship that he tried to foster between
staff and child was rather like the one he tried to foster
among the staff, i.e., delegate more responsibility and autonomy
to both.

"The atmosphere around the house, the one I tried to create,
was in actual fact a lot more free, or it was freer than
when I got there. I have very particular feelings about
children and about what one can do to help them. And one
of the things that I feel very strongly about is that if
you got a mainly adolescent group (which you will remember
Cambridge did) then your boundaries should be very well
defined. But within that, the children should have a lot

of scope to express their feelings. And that is going to
mean that at various times the children are out of control.
But only if they are allowed at times to be slightly out
of control, can they learn how to control themselves.
    I mean it's a two-way process. The way I worked it made
it far more difficult to work at Cambridge, because it's
far more demanding of staff. And a lot of criticism came
from Sylvia, and to a degree from the former superintendent,
because it wasn't run in the way Sylvia felt she wanted it
to be run, and there were difficulties there."

I feel that Alec's assessment was basically fair. Having spent
time in both units, I think that there was greater freedom of
expression among the adolescents at Cambridge than the younger
children at Oxford. It also seemed that the staff at Cambridge,
by way of this policy, had more involvement with the children,
and as a result, more work. However, I never heard them comp-
laining on this score, either on the job or retrospectively in
the taped interviews. Rather, they seemed to feel that their
greater direct involvement with the children, stemming from the
greater autonomy and responsibility delegated to them, was a
fair trade-off for more work, in that the added work was not
just more work, but more meaningful work. One might contend
that there is some ground for scepticism in accepting Alec's
account literally. After all, he is describing his own administration, and that is hardly a time to get into serious self-
criticism. However, the staff at Cambridge gave strong support
for Alec's assessment of the situation upon his arrival, and
the ways in which it changed for the better. Marilyn, the
current deputy under Ann (the new teamleader at Cambridge), had
this to say about Alec's effects upon the house.

"Sylvia used to run Cambridge when I first came; and then
Alec came and took her role and she moved up the road (to
Oxford) to become deputy superintendent. (Ray Gaines was
then still superintendent. When he left, Sylvia moved up
in the hierarchy to become acting superintendent, a position
she held until Digby came along to displace her as superintendent.) There was quite a change then at Cambridge. I
would have left if Alec hadn't come along. I found it
awful. And I mean Sylvia has got a lot of good qualities,
and is a pretty good worker; but (she) wouldn't give anybody responsibility or anything and treated you as if you
had no mind of your own. Everything has got to be done her
way. And Alec came on to me sort of democratic, and I
liked the way he worked right from the beginning.... You
were motivated to do work through fear of Sylvia's

response, rather than (because) you wanted to. And there
was much more bothering about the actual sort of domestic
side, household chores, spending money, and not getting
into things (meaningful things with the children). We have
been treated as you know (with) a sort of lack of respect,
I think."

Such are some of the differences between the two houses as they
developed over time under the leadership of Alec and Sylvia.
While some members of staff try to soft peddle these differences
as "just differences", they were in fact, at least on some
levels, the basis of active rivalries. Some among the junior
and senior staff feel that these natural divisions ought to be
maintained, in that they promote a sense of in-house identity
and a healthy competition. Others, the new superintendent among
them, felt that these differences were divisive, and ought to be
eliminated with the move to the new facility. This philosophy
held that one way to get rid of a "house divided" was to unify
both under one roof at Queen's Road, and try to promote a new
common identity that both houses could relate to. On the
question of whether or not this was a good idea, junior and
senior staff of both houses were split nearly down the middle.

JUNIOR VS. SENIOR STAFF

What of the feelings of "them and us" that exist between the
junior and senior staff? While such feelings are more widespread at Oxford, they exist at Cambridge as well. Some of the
things that junior staff felt "could have been better" within
the hierarchy were:

1. A higher level of trust between junior and senior
    staff.
2. Freer lines of communication (contingent upon the
    first condition) between junior and senior staff.
3. Fewer formal distinctions within the "hierarchy" in
    order to promote openness and democratization within
    the agency.
4. Senior staff should have provided junior staff with
    better formal structured in-house training.
5. Senior staff should have provided junior staff with
    an earlier and more intensive involvement in family
    therapy, i.e., "a case of their own".

6.   "Management" (within Social Services, but not a part
     of the in-house staff) should provide junior staff
     with more paid time for on-the-job training.
7.   The agency should provide greater involvement by the
     outside consultants in the training program.
8.   More opportunities should be made available by Social
     Services for CCOs to be subsidized in getting advanced
     social work degrees.
9.   Senior staff were keeping children too long in assess-
     ment, and denying other needy children an opportunity
     to benefit from the assessment Center's services.
10. Social Services should upgrade the standing of
     "resident childcare officer" to that of "field social-
     worker".

Formal Training

Inasmuch as we have already dealt with points one through three
in other contexts, I will begin with a consideration of the
disappointment felt by junior staff at the lack of formal in-
house training and evaluation. One relatively new childcare
worker put it this way.

Ian: "I think I enjoyed working at Oxford, but for the fact
        that I disagreed quite intensely with my member of
        (senior) staff in her way of caring for kids, and I
        disagreed, to a lesser extent, with some of the other
        staff. And I don't know, I think you find this in any
        institution, (he had worked as a volunteer in others)
        that there is a narrow-mindedness, usually because of
        the lack of training within the staff, or experience,
        or varied experience.
JJ: "What was the philosophy of childcare like at Oxford?"
Ian: "To me, the philosophy of Oxford was never really
        (stated).... I mean it was stated verbally, but it
        never really got into action.... It was meant to be
        so much involvement with families, and that was their
        basic philosophy. Whereas ... only when the parent
        absolutely demanded attention in some way, like shout-
        ing at a staff member or something like that (did they
        get any). There wasn't much going into the home (the
        child's home) and sort of thrashing things out.
        This, I think, sort of disillusioned me in a way,
        because I had been built up so much before and after
        the interview (his initial job interview) as to what
        sort of fantastic things they did here (at Oxford)

and then (all of that) sort of came to a grinding halt when
I got there and when I found that things didn't go quite
like that.... I've been here for three months now, and I
don't know what the assessment procedure is....

It was very much a case of you can learn things if you
come up and ask for it. We're (the senior staff) not going
to initiate the training program on you. We're not going
to say, here is such and such, you can take it away and
read it, or have a chat about it.... But I think that is
definitely the one thing that annoys me most of all childcare is the (lack of) training."

Nor was this lack of formal training at the agency anything new.
Shawn, a seasoned worker who had been there for three years,
notes that at the time of his arrival:

"It took me a long time to find my feet here. It took me a
long time to find out exactly what was going on. You had
a very closely knit group of experienced staff who I think,
didn't exclude you deliberately; but (because they were)
able to do everything without having to ask anybody how to
do it, you never really found out how it got done. So I
quickly found out the only way to find out anything was to
keep asking questions."

JJ: "Did you have any formal training as such on the
          job?"
Shawn: "No."

The lack of formal training applied not only to the ins and
outs of routine procedure within the agency, but to advanced
forms of formal training as well.

"You got so many people who would give their right arm to
go away on a C.Q.S.W. (the subsidized course for an
advanced social work degree), and there is just no chance.
I mean they send one (person) a year, if that (out of all
the related social service workers in the borough)."

Given the lack of opportunity for advancement through the
normal channels of formal education, workers could only
realistically expect to "come up through the ranks". This
created among the staff two conditions: (1) frustration and a
lack of incentive, and (2) an anti-intellectual "play it by
ear" approach to "on the job training" and childcare in general.

Family Therapy

In addition to the lack of formal training and educational
opportunities, there was the problem, from the junior staff's
point of view, of their lack of involvement or late involvement
in family therapy. Early in the author's stay at the Center
(in fact, before the study had formally begun) the outside
psychiatric consultant (who was the father of family therapy
at the Center and "gatekeeper" for the author)[1]* often spoke of
how novel, integral, and important the family therapy aspect of
the Center's assessment process was, not only for the children
and their families, but for the staff. I was told that all of
the staff were involved in family therapy in an active way, and
that everyone had not only a meaningful involvement in the
process, but a meaningful say in the assessment itself. While
I will deal in greater detail with this aspect of the agency in
Chapter 4, it must be said at this point that this was not so.
Many new workers did not have an active involvement in family
therapy. Indeed, many had no involvement at all. New CCOs
(as well as the author) were led to believe that doing family
therapy was an integral part of their job and were sadly
disappointed to find that it was not.

> *JJ:* "You've been at Cambridge 5 months or so now.
>   Have you been involved in family therapy yet?"
> *Philip:* "No. I got my own case last Friday; that was
>   because I made a fuss about it. I was expressing
>   lots of frustration, and I think that that was
>   due to the fact that there were ... four kids from
>   one family who were being taken (seen in family
>   therapy) by Alec, who was already involved with
>   two kids (when the other four arrived some months
>   ago) so that took out six, because he wasn't
>   about to give me the two kids he'd been working
>   with. For many reasons he was doing six out of
>   about ten kids (who resided in the house) so there
>   wasn't a lot of assessment going (on) for me or
>   Dinny (another new worker)."

In fact, Cynthia, Philip, Dinny, Ian, and a number of new
workers who were with the agency for upwards of 6 months had
had no direct involvement in family therapy. There were three
basic reasons for this. First, one senior worker frequently

---

*Superscript numbers refer to Notes at end of book.

handled not one child, but one family of children. This
severely reduced the number of cases available. Second, given
this practice, the number of cases, over the long run, was
further reduced by the fact that these children frequently
remained at the Center for assessment much longer than many
staff thought helpful, either to the children or the staff.
And third, there was, during the "transition period", a cutback,
not only in the number of new cases being seen, but in the
application of family therapy to these cases.

If many workers were concerned about their lack of active
involvement "in their own case" as things currently stood,
there was even greater anxiety regarding the future of family
therapy within the institutional confines of the new facility.
In fact, many anticipated the demise of family therapy within
the agency in the near future, something that they felt would
lead to a mass exodus of staff.

If the formal training of residential childcare officers and
their early involvement in family therapy was not all they could
have hoped for, or all that they were led to believe it would
be, it was an improvement over that state of affairs that
existed 4 or 5 years ago. Childcare prior to the introduction
of family therapy by the outside psychiatric consultants,
Alec's arrival, and Sylvia's "mellowing out" was viewed by
staff as the "dark ages". The period between the "dark ages"
and the "transition period" was seen by those who either
experienced it, or heard about it, as the "golden age". While
the more optimistic workers hoped that the move to the new
facility would bring back a new form of the "golden age", the
more pessimistic sector of the agency (by far the majority)
awaited with trepidation a new form of the "dark ages". If the
worst were realized, they expected to leave in the search for
more meaningful work, probably within the childcare network.
Indeed, a number of staff took seriously the homily "afore
warned is afore armed", and had already applied for positions
elsewhere.

Relative Deprivation

Since some aspects of junior staff's discontent with senior
staff have been dealt with elsewhere (I include among senior
staff relevant higher echelon officers within the Social
Service network), let me take as a final issue for discussion
in this section the relative deprivation in status and income
felt by "residential childcare officers" with respect to "field

social workers". Some indication of the stepchild status of
residential childcare can be found in the fact that, very few
of those obtaining advanced social work degrees go into residential social work, even though it is a real option within
the Social Service network. One seasoned worker put it this
way:

> "Residential work is very much the black sheep of the NALGO
> (National Association of Local Government Employees, the
> white collar union that residential childcare officers
> belong to) because we're not exactly white collar workers,
> but we're not quite blue collar workers, we're somewhere
> between. Especially years ago, we weren't professional, we
> weren't qualified; and white collar workers in general are
> qualified in something, even if its bashing a typewriter.
> So what the union has done to us, most of our contracts for
> example, used to be any hours required by the council, now
> we're down to a 40 hour week. It started off comparing us
> to social workers, we started off at a 48 hour week, field
> social workers on a 40 hour week. We went down to a 45
> hour week, field social workers went down to $37\frac{1}{2}$. We're
> down to 40, field social workers are down to $35\frac{1}{2}$.... So
> they (the union) still don't treat us completely correctly."

I have dealt above with some of the sources of discontent among
the junior staff, and the role that they felt the senior staff
played in creating or contributing to these problems. Not all
of the ten points previously noted were considered equally
important by CCOs. While it would be difficult to weight and
rank them, I think it safe to say that interpersonal concerns,[1]
as those related to the routine features of their job, far
outweighed status and income in importance.

STAFF AND CONSULTANTS

Let us go on now to a consideration of "them and us" as it
relates to the split between staff and consultants. One might,
if called upon to hypothesize, conjure up a long list of
reasonable natural divisions that existed between the staff
and the outside consultants. For example, the consultants
were "outsiders", or at best "marginals" to the Center, and
"insiders" have a natural antipathy for "outsiders"; the
consultants were intellectual in their approach to childcare,
the CCOs were as a group very anti-intellectual; consultants
were high status, high paid persons, while CCOs were low status,
low paid persons, who usually distrusted and resented such "out

of touch" experts; childcare workers held that the only worth-
while basis for understanding low-income families and their
problems was to have experienced a similar background one's
self, and the psychiatric consultants did not come from working
class backgrounds; and the childcare officers believed that
most of the problems experienced by the families they saw were
social in nature, i.e., resulted from a lack of education,
unemployment, or the constraints of ghetto life, while the
consultants tended to attribute most of the family's problems
to "family dynamics".

This list of plausible natural divisions between staff and
consultants and the antagonisms one might imagine them to
generate could easily be extended. However, there would be
little point in doing so, for the fact is that few, if any, of
these reasonable assumptions were binding upon the workers.
In almost every case, CCOs felt that the consultant's expertise
gave them the ability to see and understand what the worker
could not. It was generally held that "when in doubt", believe
the consultants.

One might suspect that this respect was politically motivated.
After all, the consultants were high status persons, who
exerted no small influence within the agency, and junior and
senior staff might be very reluctant to question their authority
out loud, particularly into a tape recorder. There is, I
believe, some grounds for this suspicion. However, we have
already seen that the staff did not hesitate to question everyone or anything else during these taped interviews, and many
were outspoken in doing so. With this in mind (and notwithstanding certain reservations I have on this point to be
considered later), I believe there was among the staff, for the
most part, a genuine respect for the outside psychiatric consultants and their efforts on behalf of the Center.

This does not mean that their praise was always unqualified.
Some staff preferred the personal style of one psychiatrist
over the other in leading the staff meetings or case conferences.
Most felt the consulting psychologist, who sometimes chaired
the meetings, was too non-directive. Occasionally, with regard
to a particular case, staff felt that the consultant's interpretations of the family's problems was not concrete enough.
Notwithstanding these minor reservations it was generally true
that junior and senior staff were unanimous in their apprecia-
tion of the consultant's efforts on behalf of the Center, and
held these individuals and their works in high regard.

How did the consultants view the childcare officers and/or
their efforts on behalf of the children? Here there was a wide
range of opinion. One consultant felt that there was a "tradition of care" at the Center that far exceeded the staff's
routine on-the-job obligations. Childcare officers frequently
put in many hours in excess of those they were paid for in
order to be able to act on behalf of the children or their
families. In some cases the children and their families maintained long-term friendships with the Center, that extended
years beyond any official involvements. The author, too, feels
that a "tradition of care" permeated the Center. This was in
keeping with the staff's search for and involvement in meaningful work. The Center provided this meaning, not only because
of the CCOs' involvement with helping children in need, but
because of the sense of camaraderie that developed among members
of staff. Some saw each other socially, and for many, work at
the Center had become not just a job, but a way of life. In
short, the long hours spent at the Center by CCOs, especially
the seasoned single staff, reflected not only their dedication
to the children, but constituted a significant source of
"secondary gain". This was perhaps most true of the acting
superintendent. In the opinion of the psychiatric consultant
(and the author) this dedication to the children was in many
cases a reflection of the staff's own childhood experience.

Apart from the staff's efforts on behalf of the children, one
consultant felt that it was important that the staff (Sylvia
in particular) had initiated the request for outside psychiatric
help. The consultants were not imposed upon the staff from
above by way of some higher echelon administrative directive.
Such a move, at the time it was initiated, took courage and
forethought, and reflected well in the consultant's opinion,
upon the staff.

However, if Sylvia's efforts as a caring and able childcare
worker were viewed positively by the consultants (and they were
unanimous on this point), they also saw her as the source of
much in-house friction and anxiety. In this regard, they were
in agreement with most of the staff. In fact, the consultants
saw one of their major roles within the agency as one of
mediating conflict situations between Sylvia and staff, in an
effort to keep things on an even keel. Even Sylvia's involvement with the children was a two-edged sword. The very thing
that allowed her to empathize and care for the children was
responsible for her inability to "let go". The children in her
care were not children, they were "her children". This was true
perhaps of some of the other workers as well, but not to the

same extent. Some of the implications for the agency have
already been spelled out, e.g., one worker dealt with a family
of children which left other CCOs with no cases of their own;
children stayed in care longer than necessary, and sometimes
longer than was "in the best interest of the child"; the
extension of this practice was converting the Center from a
short-term reception and assessment Center into a "long-stay
home", etc. Other aspects, as they relate to the assessment
process itself, will be dealt with in Chapter 4.

If the consultants felt that the childcare officers at the
Center were dedicated, caring, and well-meaning, some were not
so generous in their assessment of the workers' potential in
other regards. For example, one consultant thought very little
of the way staff at Oxford typically went about resolving interpersonal disputes. Rather than confronting each other with the
problem, the whole thing was heard by, and dealt with through
third party networks. The consultant put it this way.

> "Now there was one time when there was a very difficult
> situation that developed, apparently intractible in Oxford,
> a major clash of personalities. And it seemed that the
> only thing to do at that time was to see if meeting these
> two people separately would help, which proved a disaster
> because that was Oxford's way of handling it. I got sucked
> into their system, which was that everyone talked with
> other people about a third; in other words they'd try to
> triangle people in the whole time, rather than face the
> relationship (and) sort it out then and there."

Given the low level of basic trust at Oxford between junior and
senior staff, this strategy for resolving interpersonal conflict
is in no way surprising. Face-to-face, direct confrontation,
in most situations, would have been unthinkable.

The consultants saw other problems in the Center which related
more directly to the care of the children. There was, according to one consultant, two antagonistic models of care operating, sometimes simultaneously. The first was "the soft childcare worker", the other was the "hard", or "penal system worker".
From an institutional point of view, one system was too structured and did not allow for sufficient flexibility or freedom,
while the other was too unstructured and ambiguous for the
child's good. Mediating between these two camps, in an effort
to minimize the contradictions for the staff and children, was
another role consultants played within the agency. However, it

was nearly impossible to schedule workers so that one "hard" and one "soft" worker were on duty together, a combination consultants thought would be beneficial.[2] Usually "the rota" (the work schedule) only provided that one man and one woman be present at every shift; and this had less to do with childcare than the safety of the woman workers from the children, their irate parents, or outside intruders.

Apart from the different styles of childcare and the unconstructive ways in which staff sometimes sought to resolve their differences, some of the therapists offered a more personal negative assessment of the CCOs. In fact, one thought it ironic that the staff should be involved in dealing with children's problems, when the CCOs were themselves psychologically worse off than the children they treated. This psychoanalytic diagnosis was based upon the consultant's assessment of the worker's family background and childhood experiences (you will remember they were not in many cases substantially different from the children's) and the fact that most woman workers (in fact, all but one) were single. How could unmarried and childless workers know about children and/or family problems? This was, of course, the logic the workers imposed on occasion in questioning the consultant's opinions (at least among themselves), i.e., how would well educated, middle to upper class people like the consultants know anything about the problems of uneducated lower class families? One might imagine that if personal experience was the key to success, the married, middle class consultants with children might have gotten together with the unmarried lower class childcare officers and compared notes. Such a synthesis was never entertained, let alone attempted. While it is generally true that this should come as no surprise, given the status and power of psychiatrists in formal organizational settings, it is a bit peculiar that these questions were never broached at the Center. After all, it was supposed to be a novel and integral part of agency policy that everyone, junior and senior staff alike, were to be actively and meaningfully involved in the assessment process, and that all relevant parties would not only be heard, but taken seriously. With this in mind, one can only wonder why the consultants, who were experts at keeping interpersonal lines of communication open, were so reticent to do so in this case. It seems to the author that notwithstanding the high regard in which the staff held the consultants, there was, at least at some levels, a reciprocal lack of basic trust in this sector of the agency as well.

Finally, in the opinion of some consultants, the dedication of
the single women on staff to the children, and the feeling that
the children were "our children" stemmed less from the CCOs'
past background and level of empathy, than from the psychoanalytic notion that these were surrogate children who symboli-
cally filled a void for the women workers in their unconscious
desire for motherhood. This, coupled with a "separation
anxiety" that some women workers experienced as a result of
their own childhood, was from the consultant's perspective, the
reason that they had so much trouble "letting go" of the children in their care. The above was viewed as an unhealthy state
of affairs, not only for the children, but the staff.

This psychiatric interpretation, like the one above, was never
dealt with openly. Nor should they be viewed as "only abstrac-
tions". They constituted for the consultants, an understanding
and explanation of the level and kind of care the children were
likely to receive, and why. As a consequence, they are important, not only because "if men define situations as real, they
are real in their consequences",[3] but more specifically because
the private assessments of some of the consultants, regarding
staff's potential to act "in the best interest of the child"
were directly at odds with their public evaluations of the
staff in the staff meetings. This lack of candor on the part
of the consultants contributed, I believe to the larger problem
of the lack of formal training and open communication within
the agency.

I have already dealt with the suspiciously universal high
regard the staff had toward the consultants. When I mentioned
to one of the consultants in the interview that no member of
staff had questioned the efforts of any of the consultants, he
said, "Well, that's a criticism of the institution, then,
isn't it? It should be possible." The irony seems to be that
I rarely heard the consultants publically question the efforts
of the staff. In fact, there seemed to be a reciprocal tacit
understanding among the staff and consultants to maintain a
conspiracy of silence. This position can be reformulated to
read that staff and consultants had tacitly agreed to form a
mutual admiration society. If this made the work more pleasant,
it contributed very little to making it more effective or
meaningful.

CHILDREN AND STAFF

As previously indicated, the nature of interaction among children and staff varied somewhat from house to house. The approach of the staff at Oxford might be characterized as firm but friendly, accompanied by a pronounced element of "distancing". This was envoked by staff in the name of avoiding status ambiguity and maintaining a professional posture. Such a posture, while it provided for better control and a structurally consistent in-house policy, also went a long way toward accentuating the "them and us" nature of staff-child relationships.

The approach at Cambridge was somewhat different. It was more friendly, less firm, and had a lower level of distancing. This produced a more flexible, but less structured or predictable environment, and a lower level of "us and them" feeling between children and staff.

How did the children relate to the staff? The children's approach at Oxford may be described as cautious, courteous, and helpful. The children's approach at Cambridge was more open and friendly, but less courteous, and/or predictably helpful. House rules at Cambridge were more often breached by the children with impunity. In keeping with the soft-hard model of social work, there were more "softies" than "hardies" at Cambridge. Let us now consider these features in greater detail and their implications for childcare.

Natural Antagonisms

There were in both houses two distinct sub-cultures — the staff and the children. The "consciousness of kind" and feeling of "we-ness" that defined these two groups was not only different but frequently antagonistic.[4] The children saw their role as one of maximizing freedom, while the staff (no matter how "loose") were always aware of the need for control.

While these natural antagonisms between child and parent may be found in any family setting, there was a major difference in the configuration it took at the Center. To begin with, the childcare workers were not the children's parents, they were their keepers. In this sense, there was a natural antagonism toward staff, which staff had to overcome in order to be able to relate meaningfully with the child. Parents are not initially confronted by this natural division. The fact that children begin by loving their parents, and must learn to hate

or dislike them, as opposed to disliking the staff from the
start, and having to learn to like or abide them, puts the staff
in a very disadvantaged position, vis a vis their relationship
with the children. Add to this the fact that many children did
not wish to be at the Center, and were a captive audience, and
one can see how antagonisms between children and staff were
unavoidable. While antagonisms were not always overt, the
ever-present stressful "vibes", especially at Oxford, were
evidence of their covert presence. The untoward consequences
of these relationships were further compounded by the staff
being the final arbitor of what was "in the best interest of
the child". The child was not viewed as an active member of
the assessment team, and had no voice in the Center's recommendation to the Magistrate, and very little influence upon the
Magistrate's final decision regarding his/her future placement.

With this in mind, it is perhaps not surprising to find that
while the staff worked hard to make the "house" a "home", and
get the child to view the staff as "family", they were not very
successful in this undertaking from the children's point of
view. While some CCOs viewed the house as a home and the staff
and children as a family, the children were always well aware
of the fact that they were not a part of a family, but an
institution. In short, if some of the staff felt some of the
children were "our children", none of the children believed
that some of the staff were "our parents", or that Oxford or
Cambridge was "our home". This is not to say that the children
at Cambridge or Oxford were mistreated, they were not, or that
some of the children there were not glad to be there given
their options. But glad or not, one had the distinct impression
that the children in both houses did not feel "at home" there,
and that this feeling was more pronounced among the children at
Oxford.

It was not only the children who recognized these subcultural
differences. Most of the staff were also aware (on one level
or another) of this unbrideable schism, an active rhetoric to
the contrary notwithstanding. One childcare officer talking
about the impending move to the new facility, put it this way:

> "There's nothing homey about Cambridge at all, or even
> Oxford really. You make the best of what you can. Of
> course people were hoping for something homey after those
> two places, and we're not getting it (with the move to the
> new facility). I think some people are going to feel that
> they don't want to work there."

In keeping with the fact that, when in doubt, the children
presumed against the good intentions of the workers for the
reasons outlined above, there is the question of what the staff
did to overcome this initial negativity. Basically, they tried
to relate to the children's problems and establish at the very
least, an element of trust. This was attempted at the Center
in much the same way as one attempts it elsewhere, i.e., through
a combination of words and deeds. These efforts took two basic
forms. First, the CCO tried to treat the child fairly within
the bounds of the house rules (which the child learns early on,
and is constantly reminded of) and secondly, the worker seeks
to engage the child in play or other meaningful activities.
How well do these efforts succeed? If we mean by this, do the
children place more trust in the staff than they do in their
peers, then we must conclude that the staff's efforts are not
very successful. However, given the natural divisions noted
above, such a definition of trust is more than one could hope
for. On a more realistic level, some staff succeeded better
than one might have expected in "establishing rapport". Apart
from the inherent problems given above, there were others that
mitigated against the staff succeeding in such an undertaking.

Let us begin a discussion of these problems with a consideration
of "consistency" as it relates to the staff's words and deeds.
There is a psychological literature that deals with the nature
of interactions within the families of schizophrenic children.
One view has it that the parents of schizophrenic children give
the child contradictory messages, a circumstance that places
the child in a "double bind", i.e., the child is placed in a
no-win situation with respect to his/her being able to please
the parent.[5] The constraints of these contradictory communications preclude the possibility of the child acting appropriately.
The therapeutic remedy for this is to arrange matters in family
therapy so that the parents recognize the impossible demands
they are placing upon the child. With this insight, the
parents are then called upon to stop acting inconsistently (and
requiring the child to act that way), and start acting in a
clear and consistent fashion toward the child, so that he may
reciprocate in kind.

Imagine the extent of this problem within the Center. First
there is the old chestnut, "we're all different", i.e., no two
people perceive or react to their environment in exactly the
same way. All parents, of course, have this problem to overcome
(to one extent or another) in order to act consistently toward
their child. Imagine how this problem is compounded when the
child does not have two parents, but seven or eight, as is the

case at Oxford or Cambridge. Now add to this the "play it by
ear" approach of staff toward the children that stems from
their lack of prior or on-the-job training. Couple this to the
different general approaches to childcare taken by the two
houses, and the fact that the same child may be moved from one
house to the other during his or her stay, or be placed in one
house on one occasion, and the other another time. Add to this
an active turnover in staff at the lower levels, and the daily
changes in staffing, and you have an almost impossible situation
with respect to the staff's efforts to act consistently toward
the child.. This says nothing of the individual variation
between one worker and another to act or talk consistently in
the course of any one shift.

In addition to the staff's search for consistency in their
dealings with the children, there is the problem of child-staff
relationships at play. Staff have not only the obligation of
caring for the children, but are under constant pressure to
entertain them as well. While play situations provide another
important avenue for the worker in his/her attempt to overcome
the child's initial lack of trust, it is one that the staff in
both houses seemed not to pursue with much enthusiasm. There
are a number of reasons for this. One important one is the
lack of energy the staff feels due to understaffing and/or
"long days" (a situation where one staff covers for another by
working a double shift). One childcare officer expressed it
this way:

> "Well, one of the things I think we need to do much more
> of is group work with the kids. I mean, usually when I'm
> on (duty) I try to get them out to do something, when there
> are 5 or 6 of them; and at least it gets them to interact
> which is better than just sitting in the sitting room and
> bitching at each other.... the atmosphere just sort of
> builds up and builds up and soon something blows, and it's
> usually one of the younger kids that cops it first. I
> think there's not enough getting them out and doing things.
> But at the same time, I understand, because I do it myself
> — the feeling of no, I don't want to do that, you know, I
> don't want to move, because everyone is so bloody tired at
> the moment, because there's a lot of hours worked. I
> managed to get 5 of them out this morning (to the park) to
> play football, and they enjoyed that. I had to shout at one
> of them before we went, because he was being his typical
> lethargic self. So I called him "a goddamn, lazy son of
> a bitch". He certainly played football ... which I'm quite
> pleased about. It was the first time I've actually seen

him play or do anything.... I mean he usually just buggers
off by himself, and doesn't do anything, just sits there."

In fact, while on the unit, many children spent a lot of time
"just sitting". The younger children were more resourceful
than the older ones at keeping busy. Both spent a lot of time
watching "telly". However, the older children at Cambridge,
because they were older, could more often seek diversion outside
the unit, either by themselves or in the company of a CCO, while
the younger children at Oxford usually busied themselves play-
ing in the social room or in the enclosed yard adjacent to it.
The problem of the staff's general reluctance to initiate and/
or sustain play with the children was compounded by a lack of
toys. This was made worse by the fact that children frequently
played inside, due to bad weather. Even in light of the
Center's tight budget, and the fact that the children typically
destroyed games in a matter of minutes, there was a real need
in both units for more play things.

The net result of all of these conditions was an easily
initiated and sustained set of sub-cultures that led to sharp
"them and us" feelings between the children and staff. Given
these circumstances, the reader might wonder how the CCOs
succeed even minimally in establishing and sustaining meaningful relationships with the children. First the staff did play
with the children, and did take them on outings, even if it was
not as often as the children might have wished. But apart from
these activities, there were many others throughout the day
where the staff and children interacted. For example, the
staff took their meals with the children, got them ready for
school (Bob drove them there at 9 am, and returned them at
3.30 pm), gave the smaller ones their baths, changed their
clothes when they soiled them, and put them to bed. The
children also helped the staff by cleaning up after meals, and
sometimes assisted in the preparation of "tea", or in shopping.
How successful staff were during these times at relating to the
children varied from worker to worker. In order for the reader
to get a better idea of these activities, and how they were
scheduled, we have offered the following edited transcript:

> *JJ:*　　OK. Now then there was the routine of going
> 　　　　through the day. Did you wanna do a run-through
> 　　　　on that?
> *Marilyn:*　"Well, our morning starts at half past seven.
> 　　　　Within an hour you got to get them (the children)
> 　　　　all up, breakfast, (clean) the bedrooms, the beds
> 　　　　made, and all this sort of thing. It's generally

rushing about, there might be letters to write to
send to the school and getting the dinner menu out
and all this sort of thing. Anyway, you have to
have them out in an hour (and on their way to the
regular school or special tutorials). When they're
gone there's the cleaning up from that, general,
just duties. On different days we do specific
things that need doing, like laundry, and menus
and shopping, and bedroom cupboards, and all sort
of general things. I do a lot of, in the morning,
a lot of phone-calls, contacting social workers,
what's happened the night before, or hurrying
people up about placements (for the children) and
maybe talking to teachers — something happened at
school the day before, something like that. And
(then there is) general maintenance, contacting
people ... then there's just sort of the general
run of the house, like housewife stuff. And set
the tables for lunch."

JJ: "You have to shop the food yourself? Figure out
menus, or what?"

Marilyn: "Yeah. At the moment, because we're at Grandview
Road, we put in the orders and Bob (the driver)
collects it, there's still odds and ends to go
and get though. But when you're at Cambridge,
you got to do the shopping yourself."

JJ: "Right."

Marilyn: "And if there's little kids about, you normally
take them with you. The other ones are at school.
You normally have a couple at home, one of them
might be ill, we spend time with them during the
day as well. You got the tutorial kids coming in
for lunch, between quarter past twelve and half
(past) one, and normally after lunch you have
quite a session. When the tutorial kids are in,
we normally have quite a session talking after
dinner before they go back to tutorial (special
class, not a part of the normal school system)
always some sort of topic comes up, or I'll often
do sort of dancing with them and that, after
lunch. We have music on and we dance around. At
Cambridge we all, every lunch time, we used to do
that with Larry and Brian, (two of the teenage
children) we used to have a dance session for
half an hour. And there's normally people (to
visit) say Richard from the youth club, Bill,
who's a teacher, has a stop (by). One of those

might come for lunch, and they might want to see
you or Linda, the tutorial teacher, to discuss
some sort of problem with the kids; we have
different people in and they discuss things.
And then you're getting them off to school, and
you might, you know, have some of them in the
afternoon, some of them go to school say half the
day. You do things with them, getting all prepared for tea (around 4.30), you have the tea (a
light evening meal) to make yourself, tables to
set, and there's all different shopping (to do).
You might go out to the park and take them (the
children) out for a walk if you got the young
ones."

JJ: "And the kids come back for tea about what time?"
Marilyn: "Half three, quarter to four. And then you spend,
normally at half three to four is "change over",
where the staff's coming on (for a change of
shift) and you say what's been happening and give
information (about the children) during the half
hour. And then from four o'clock to five, I mean,
you're (booked) solid, the kids will never leave
you alone the first hour when they're in. You
have tea with them, and that normally takes sort
of an hour, to clear up and start organizing
what's happening in the evening, and who's going
out and all this sort of thing, getting them off
to family meetings, and.... And you spend the
evening — do different things, watch the telly
(TV) or go out somewhere."

JJ: "You take the kids places?"
Marilyn: "Yeah, swimming, ice skating, like that."
JJ: "That's usually evening stuff?"
Marilyn: "Yeah. Or a lot will be happening all in the
holidays when we have them all at home — weekends."
JJ: "Aha, on weekends."
Marilyn: "And you spend a lot of time talking to them of
different problems, personal problems, school, day-
to-day things, especially when you put them to
bed. And reading stories you spend a lot of time
(with) the younger ones, getting supper (and)
washing up (the dishes and the children). And
evening, that's a nice time in a way, you can get
quite sort of close to kids, talking about things
and you can sort of guide or help (them) or whatever, and you can often feel you're doing more
then, talking about things (that concern them).

At the end of the day when you're feeling a bit domestic, it's nice when they come to you, with something (of importance to them)."

JJ: "In the evenings? When they get talking more about their day and their problems?

Marilyn: "Yeah. And the kids talk more to each other as well, cause normally it's dark, and at bedtime and things in their room, a lot of them sit in their bedrooms and they talk together — while they're all in bed — about different things."

JJ: "What do they talk about?"

Marilyn: "... sort of fairness stuff, being fair, and you know when they're being helped, money, buying clothes, the general running of the place or questioning our rules, or difficulties of living with people, all different people. And what's going to be happening to them, why are they here, when are they going and where are they going."

JJ: "What can you tell them about any of that, when and where they're going?"

Marilyn: "As much as you know. But we're often in the dark, as well as them; it's a very difficult time, so many unknowns. And even if you know exactly where they should go, there aren't many sorts of places (like the one you want for the child) that are available."

STAFF AND PARENTS

We have presented above some of the natural antagonisms confronting the staff in their efforts to establish a trusting relationship with the children, and how they sought to overcome them. Let us now consider the feeling of "us and them" that exists between the staff and parents.

Because of the composition of the children at the Center at the time of the study, more parents visited their children at Oxford than at Cambridge. These visits, while they were usually uneventful, were at other times quite dramatic. In nearly all cases, it is the mother who visits. This was true not only because some fathers worked (for some were unemployed and mothers sometimes worked as well) or because in some cases the father was no longer with the family, but rather because of the father's reluctance to come to the Center.

Visits typically took the following form. The parent or
parents would seat themselves in the social room, usually
before the television and totally ignore the children and staff.
In an effort to be polite, staff would offer them a cup of tea,
or depending on the hour, something to eat, which they usually
accepted. Their child might from time to time make incursions
into the parent's social space where a word or two was exchanged,
and then each went about their own business as though the
other had not existed. These exchanges usually took one of two
forms. The parents brought the child "treats" in the form of
sweets, or the parent told the child to behave itself, and stop
being a nuisance. The demeanor of the parent toward the staff
was usually civil but distant. Sometimes this low-key affect
erupted in the course of a visit and the staff were threatened
with kitchen knives, screamed and/or cursed at, or subject to
verbal threats. Such occurrences did not happen often, but
when they did they were the topic of serious discussion among
staff, not only informally, but in staff meetings. Other times
the same parent would be conciliatory and try to be overly
helpful.

How could one account for these dramatic mood swings? Like the
actions of most people, such behaviors on the part of the parent
or parents were in response to their personal circumstances, as
they understood them. In particular, there was the real threat
that the agency would try to keep the child from the parents on
a permanent basis by recommending to the court that the child
be placed in "care". The parent's understanding of the child's
status in the course of these proceedings changed constantly on
the basis of the information they received in "family conferences", through the "grapevine", by way of "vibes" received in
the course of their visit, or from what their children told
them. In reaction to their changing assessments of the threat
of losing their child, or sometimes what they took to be
inadequate care at the Center, parents adopted coping strategies
in an effort to change things for the better. Remembering the
disadvantaged position of power that the parents operated from
(the Center usually already had a care order) the parent(s)
could only vacillate between conciliatory and rebellious
behavior in an effort to influence the Center in their decision.
This they did in extremes, and frequently out of desperation,
for extreme circumstances (the threat of losing one's child)
frequently calls forth extreme measures. Some indication of
the political and legal edge that the agency has over the parent
in such proceedings can be had from an article in a social work
journal (*Community Care*, 1 February, 1978, page 17).

"More than 100,000 children are now in care in England and Wales, either because of civil care proceedings or offences they committed. All of them have been processed through the juvenile courts who grant care orders to the local authorities.

There is a growing concern with the way in which care orders are made; with what is seen as inadequate representation of parents and children and lack of competence and expertise of some social workers, lawyers and magistrates, especially in view of the considerable amount and complexity of childcare legislation.

The concern about natural justice is that much stronger because the families involved are those least well equipped to fight back against the might of the local authority. Robert Holman, former professor of social administration and now a field social worker, has said that about 98 percent of children in care come from the most deprived strata of society. Is this perhaps yet another form of inequality suffered by them?

According to DHSS figures on 1976 admissions to care (quoted in *Social Trends*), the most common single reason for placing a child in care under Section I of the 1948 Children Act, is "incapacity of parent or guardian". What many people would question is how the criteria for deciding this incapacity are chosen, and by whom.

Harry Fletcher, a social worker at the National Council for One Parent Families, emphasised that too often one-parent families come under the category of "inadequate". Professor Roy Parker of Bristol University has estimated that at least 75 percent of all children who appear in civil care proceedings, have been or are now from one-parent families.

So are too many children being taken into care? The charges against the system are many and very serious. It is suggested that parents' rights (and, therefore, their children's) are being eroded; they do not automatically receive legal aid if they want to contest the local authority's decision to place their child in care. Even if the parents are represented, ask the critics, what is the standard of the average lawyer in this case? It would seem that until recently, the legal profession has overlooked the importance of this very complex area of childcare legislation."

How were the parent's efforts at coping viewed by the staff?
When the parent waxed pleasant and helpful, the staff "saw
through this" and recognized a "cover up", i.e., the parent's
less than honest attempt to influence the Center to return the
child home. When the parent became abrasive or hostile, they
were showing "their true selves", but not one that the staff
could abide, deal with, or condone. Either way, the parent's
efforts miscarried in their attempt to have a positive influence,
either upon the staff or their recommendations to the court.
It was also true that "difficult parents" earned this label by
making trouble, and no one likes trouble. As a result, the
staff in self-defense sought to stear clear of "difficult
parents". This, of course, did little to open the lines of
communication necessary to resolve the conflict. "Difficult
parents", like "difficult kids", were seen as agency failures,
and treated with avoidance, or an effort on the part of staff
to tactfully route them elsewhere. This similarity in the way
that staff handled "difficult kids" and "difficult parents" and
their justification for it can be seen in the following remarks.
One childcare officer addressing Falicia's case (you will remember
from an earlier reference that Falicia and Joan were considered
failures) had this to say:

> "And the staff was feeling that she's (Falicia) got to go.
> I certainly said it very strongly to Sylvia, and Sylvia said
> OK, I agree with you, we can't do anything (for her). I
> mean my philosophy really is that if we have failed to make
> contact with the kid you know, she shouldn't be here anymore.
> Apart from any other considerations, she's holding up a bed
> that someone else could use, and possibly more than she
> can."

Another childcare officer had this to say about the staff's
routine handling of "difficult parents".

> "... as soon as a difficult parent was sort of come up
> against, a lot of people (staff) tried their level best not
> to do any work with them ...".

One put it this way:

> "So after the initial home interviews and psychological
> testing and everything else, there is a lot of contact with
> the kids, but hardly any with the parents."

Parents, as well as their children, were viewed by staff as a
potential control problem. Contingency plans were made about
how to summon the police in emergencies, or deal directly with
irate parents. In most cases, staff felt a bigger threat from
the visiting parents than from the children, not only because
of the direct threats to their person, but because parental
visits were usually viewed by staff as detrimental to the child
as well. For example, parents "bribing" their children in an
effort to win their favor, was seen as disruptive, and only
served to undo the good that the agency had accomplished while
the child was in their care. There was the additional problem
that much parental behavior was viewed by staff as "paranoid
behavior", i.e., parents exhibited suspicion toward the staff
in what the staff viewed as an irrational or undue concern for
their child's well being. However, on one level such suspicions
were not unfounded. While the staff were not abusing the children (they were, in fact, well cared for) it was not unreasonable
for parents to suspect abuse. The daily newspapers were full of
unsavory accounts. For example, the London *Times* (Friday,
23 December, 1977, page 3) caption reads, "Public inquiry
condemns harsh and insensitive treatment of children at assessment center." The story goes on to report:

> "Salford Social Service Committee yesterday accepted the
> report of a public inquiry, published earlier in the day,
> saying that outmoded institutional practices and insensitive
> and harsh treatment of children at the Moorfield Observation
> and Assessment Center in the city should cease.
> The inquiry was set up in May this year after allegations
> of harsh treatment of children 'held' at the centre awaiting
> decisions on future accommodation or treatment.
> One of the allegations was that a boy had been picked up
> by his head and ears by the warden, who with the deputy
> warden (his wife), had been sent on leave since the inquiry
> began. The social service committee decided yesterday that
> the warden should return to his post.
> The inquiry report says it was understood that instructions
> had already been given to end the outmoded practices and
> harsh treatment, including corporal punishment, compulsory
> cold baths, and forcing of children to eat unwanted food.
> It found proved allegations that a boy was picked up by
> his head and ears by the warden "in totally unacceptable
> circumstances"; that on a few occasions boys were punched or
> kicked (this was not a regular feature of the regime but is
> totally unacceptable), and that slapping and slippering of
> boys was a regular, but not frequent feature of the regime."

There is another defense of the parent's apparent "paranoid
tendencies". The fact is that the Center did sometimes conspire
against the parents, "for their own good" and for the "good of
the child". This conspiracy took the following form. Care
orders were sometimes sought, not only in order to have sufficient time in which to assess the child, or to keep the child
for relatively long periods of time at the Center for his/her
own good (when this was seen as the best of a series of bad
options); but also to secure a position of power from which to
threaten the parents with the loss of their child if they didn't
improve their efforts (as the agency defined them) to act in
"the best interest of the child". Parents sometimes accused
the agency of this practice, at which point the agency replied
with some reference to the parent's "paranoia". The following
is a verbatim account of this practice by one of the residential
childcare officers.

> "One of the advantages of sometimes having a full care order
> is that if you're working with the family, when the child
> comes into care, you take responsibility away from them
> (the parents). And when you're working with a family and
> things are looking like the child may get home again, you're
> handing them (the parents) back the responsibility. But
> the big chunk of responsibility is to say, right, we're
> going to give you responsibility for yourselves and Mary
> (the child), we're revoking the care order.... So you get
> it (the responsibility) all back (if you act responsibly)."

Such covert behavior by the agency was not done vindictively or
with the intent of punishing either the parent or the child.
Rather it was an altruistically motivated strategy intended to
encourage safe and responsible behavior by the parent. However,
good intentions aside, such practices were less than honest and
to the extent they were recognized or suspected by the parents,
it gave them good grounds for their "paranoia".[6]

We have outlined above some of the natural stresses between
parents and staff and traced their origins. Having done so,
we will move on now to a consideration of the assessment process
and its effect upon the child.

4

A House Decided:
The Assessment Process

At the end of Chapter 1 we outlined eight different commonly
invoked forms of recommendations that the agency passed on to
the magistrate in an effort to assist and guide him in acting
"in the best interest of the child".

1. Return the child to his/her parents, subject to certain
   constraints imposed by the court, and monitored by the
   field social worker.
2. Place the child in a "long term care facility".
3. Foster home placement.
4. Boarding school.
5. Special therapeutic setting.
6. Training school.
7. Place children 18 or over in a "hostel".
8. Leave the child in the care of the reception and
   assessment Center for relatively long periods of time.

How did the agency and staff decide which of these options to
choose? The "gloss" on this was that the decision was the outcome of the assessment process.[1]* This was also outlined at
the end of Chapter 1, and in order to reorient the reader and
refresh his memory, is presented again in abbreviated form
below.

1. A "remand" or "care order" must be acquired from the
   courts.
2. A field social worker is assigned to the case.
3. A professional meeting is called.
4. A family meeting is initiated.

---

*Subscript numbers refer to Notes at end of book.

5. The child is given a battery of psychological tests.
6. The staff discusses the daily progress of the child at "handover time".
7. Teacher's report on the child's progress in school.
8. Case conferences are initiated involving the staff, psychiatric consultants, field social worker, and parents.
9. A staff conference (or conferences) is called, where reports from all relevant parties are considered and a final assessment is made.
10. The "placement officer" assesses the availability of real options for placement.
11. The recommendations are forwarded to the court.
12. These may be accepted by the parents or contested in court.
13. There is a final outcome and the child is "placed".

These thirteen steps were generally subsumed under four main stages: (1) Staff Meeting, (2) Family Meeting, (3) Report Construction, and (4) Case Conference (final conference). Let us now consider in some detail how this scenario is played out. This analysis will be based upon the author's participant observation in staff meetings, the taped interviews with CCOs, and an analysis of official case records. Inasmuch as I was not privy to "family meetings", or the psychiatric home interviews, I will rely to some extent for this material upon the information of others who had recently studied the Center.[*] It is interesting to note that while invoking different sociological methods than that of the author, this study found, through conversational analysis, many of the same formal features of the assessment process to be described in this work.

USING THE PAST TO RECONSTRUCT THE PRESENT

The immediate assessment team composed of junior and senior staff and the consultants, invoked the same general procedures for understanding the present and anticipating the future as any competent layman, i.e., reference to the past. Inasmuch as it is generally believed by laymen and practitioners that current social and psychological events are causally related to prior events, the search for understanding begins with the reconstruction of the child's family history. In this under-

---

[*]Philip T. Davis, "Interpretive Strategies in the Assessment of Juveniles", unpublished B.Litt. Thesis, Oxford University.

taking, the staff have many allies. Families rarely enter the assessment process without some sort of "official" social work, psychiatric, psychological, school, or police record preceding them. These various slices of official history serve as a convenient fast-food way for the assessment team to bake a passable biographical, social-psychological pie. The standard social work referral form given below is one example of this sort of data.

When we realize that any bit of information is subject to numerous interpretations, and that there are many bits of information within the official records, the question arises — how did the assessment team decide which information is relevant and how to agree on its interpretation?

REFERRAL FORM

THIS PAGE MUST BE COMPLETED IN FULL

REFERRAL FORM

Name of Child:

Date of Birth:

Address:

Parents:

Marital Status:

Address:

Religion:

School:

Headmaster:

Tel. No.

SECTION UNDER WHICH HELD:	FOR USE OF RECEPTION UNIT ONLY
Supervision Order:	Date of Admission:
Care Order:	Agreed By:
Place of Safety:	Received By:
Other:	

ASSESSMENT REQUIRED: - Yes/No

To be used by whom:

For what purpose:

Social Worker:

Area: Tel. No.:

Senior Social Worker:

REFERRAL FORM

THE FOLLOWING QUESTIONNAIRE IS FOR ASSESSMENT PURPOSES ONLY AND MUST BE COMPLETED AS FULLY AS POSSIBLE

Reason for Referral:

Events which led to Referral:

CONDITIONS AT HOME AT TIME OF REFERRAL:

In General:

Relationship with Mother:

Relationship with Father:

Relationship with Siblings:

Other Important People in Child's Life:

Child's Behavior at Home:

Does it seem: (Possible, Impossible, Important)
    to Return Child Home in (Immediate, Distant)
    Future

ANY KNOWN EMOTIONAL DISORDER OR PHYSICAL DISABILITY (Bed-Wetting,
    Hearing, Vision, etc.)

RELEVANT MEDICAL INFORMATION (including recent illnesses or
    hospitalization)

CHILD'S GENERAL PRACTITIONER: Tel. No.:

PAST COURT APPEARANCE:

Date of Hearing:

Offence:

Decision:

REFERRAL FORM

CONDITIONS AT SCHOOL AT TIME OF REFERRAL:

Attendance:

Academic Work:

Behavior:

Other Schools Attended (if known):

Does it Seem (Possible, Impossible, Uncertain) to Return Child
    to School in (Immediate, Distant) Future:

Specific Questions about Ability to do School Work:

PREVIOUS PLACEMENTS AND/OR AGENCIES INVOLVED:
    (please include reason for placement)

WHAT TYPE OF INTERVENTION HAS BEEN ATTEMPTED:

SPECIFIC QUESTIONS YOU WOULD LIKE ANSWERED:

WHAT DECISIONS WILL BE AFFECTED BY THE ASSESSMENT:

HAS THE CHILD EVER BEEN ASSESSED BEFORE:

BY WHOM:

    When:

    For what Reason:

STAFF MEETING

Staff meetings may be characterized by a situation akin to that found in voting studies. While everyone gets to vote, there are some people who are more influential than others in deciding how people vote. These are called "opinion leaders".[2] The assessment team's opinion leaders were the consultants. This analogy is easily extended to the role of foreman in jury studies.[3] Like the foreman, consultants organized staff meetings, decided which topics to treat and in which order, how much time would be given to each member of staff during presentations, interpreted, clarified, and summarized discussions at different points in the meeting, served as role models, and formulated the final recommendation to the court.

The consultant was influential in other ways as well. As previously noted, data does not speak for itself but needs to be interpreted. The interpretation of the consulting psychiatrist was psychoanalytic. This professional frame of reference helped the consultants to select "relevant" information from the official records, and provide it with what they understood to be a meaningful interpretation. Given the high status of the consultants, and the high esteem in which they were held by the staff, they also offered a basis for getting consensus, i.e., their interpretation was likely to prevail.[4] We have noted in earlier chapters the staff's position that "when in doubt, believe the consultants".

Given the staff's lack of formal training, and the consultant's high level of expertise, one might easily conclude that while not overly democratic, such a decision-making process was at least rational, that is, it provided for the best possible outcome for the child, given the available information and assessibility of options.

Alas, here too there is much room for scepticism. The fact is that of all the members of the assessment team, the consultants had the least contact with the child, the least firsthand knowledge of the child's behavior or beliefs and usually the least secondhand knowledge of the child, by way of the official records. In fact, it was not unusual for a consultant to forget the child's name, age, or family background, or to be mistaken about which child was under discussion. Notwithstanding all this, they felt in no way hindered in formulating an authoritative version of the child's problems and how the agency could best act to resolve them.

This is not to say that junior and senior staff had nothing to say in the matter or that the consultants were overbearing. While some consultants were more "structured" than others in directing professional meetings, most junior staff felt that they (to return to the jury model) all "had their day in court". While this was the personal assessment of the staff, it did not coincide with the author's observations. In fact, most junior staff either had very little to say or chose to say very little in staff meetings. The latter would be in keeping with junior staff's position regarding their relationship to senior staff, i.e., when it came to debating controversial issues, it was held that "discretion was the better part of valor". As such, "consensus" in decision-making was more often than not indicative less of agreement than deferment. The need for consensus will receive greater consideration in our discussion of "reports".

There were other constraints upon who said what in staff meetings, apart from those that were self imposed. The consultants gave about an hour and a half a week to the Center. A good portion of this time you will recall was spent in dealing not with the children's problems, but with staff's. Under the circumstances, the parsimonious use of time became a matter of practical necessity. Once again, how best to use the time allotted was usually left to the personal discretion of the consultant. While their appraisal of which topics were important or relevant were not always unilaterally decided, and depending upon who chaired the meeting the staff was sometimes polled for topics of discussion; such forays in democracy did little to alter the fact that the chairperson usually decided the day's agenda.

It was also true of the decision-making process that in keeping with bureaucratic modus operandi, there was a built-in conservatism to swift action. A decision on current problems was usually deferred to future meetings. Nothing was done in haste. This deferment policy worked wonders. Many current problems evaporated, either through a change in circumstance or a lapse of memory. While offering temporary relief from a plethora of problems and the lack of time or resources to deal with them, this approach produced others. Over the long run there was the general feeling among staff, that important issues were never really resolved, and that there was very little anyone could do about it.

We have seen that the general orientation invoked by the
psychiatrist was psychoanalytic and how this frame of reference
was used to interpret which things about the case history were
important and why. What were some of the things that the
consultants and staff felt were important to know about the
child? The standard referral form gives us some indication,
e.g., religion, conditions at home, any known emotional disorder,
relevant medical information, conditions at school, or previous
placements, were all used to organize and understand the
children's past in a standardized fashion. All of this material
could then be used by the consultant and staff to help explain
the "family dynamics", and how the family dynamics served to
initiate and/or perpetuate the conditions found on the form
under the various headings.

The above gives some indication of how time was organized and
utilized during the professional meetings. Among other things,
this first stage of the assessment process was used to decide
whether or not to involve the family in the assessment process,
and if so, whether the family should come to the Center, or
the assessment team go to them.

THE FAMILY MEETING

The family meeting, like the professional meeting, was used as
a way of gathering information on the child's present and past
problems. However, instead of relying primarily upon secondary
sources of data such as the referral form and other official
records, the family meeting was called as a way of assessing
firsthand the nature of family dynamics, what the presenting
problem is, how it is viewed by the various family members, and
on the basis of all this, and prior information, to find some
therapeutic way to change old family patterns for the better.
This ideally would resolve both the child's and family's problems, and allow them to be reunited.

The official function of family meetings, taken from a reprint
of a publication by one of the consultants and outlining the
assessment process at the Center, is given as follows:

> "at the ... assessment Center the use of family meetings
> with adolescents in care has proved invaluable in the
> process of the assessment and placement of troubled children.
> As seen in the material (from a case presented in the
> article) ... work with the entire family reveals hitherto
> unknown dynamics of family life which are essential in

planning for a child's future, and also allows the family
members to re-experience deeply buried often terribly pain-
ful feelings, which underlie the causes of the adolescent
coming into care. The work of the field (social) worker
and residential staff (CCO) is essential for the successful
execution of this particular model of assessment."

Negotiating Reality

This process of defining the "presenting complaint" and the
search for its origin can be seen as a case of "negotiated
reality".[5] These negotiations follow a line similar to those
found in other forms of doctor-patient interactions and are
based upon similar sets of assumptions. These can be outlined
as follows: The doctor (practitioner or other expert) is able
by way of his expertise to understand the patient's problem
better than the patient; if the patient's assessment of their
problem does not coincide with the doctor's, the doctor is seen
to have the authoritative version. If the patient comes to
accept the doctor's version of reality and does as he prescribes,
he is defined by the doctor as a "good patient", if not, a "bad
patient". "Bad patients" who are adamant in maintaining their
position are with time defined as a "bad risk", i.e., someone
the doctor (through no fault of his own/or the state of the art)
is unable to help. And, finally, the patient does not tell the
doctor what is wrong, or what to do about it, the doctor tells
the patient.[6]

This process presents certain logical peculiarities. If the
doctor knows your problem, and his understanding of it is
independent of anything you know or think, what is the basis of
negotiation in the process of negotiating reality. The fact is,
of course, in most cases, the doctor (therapist) does not and
cannot know what your problem is until you tell him. In fact,
his being able to tell you is contingent upon your being able to
tell him your symptoms, prior medical history, how you feel
about things, etc. One's "definition of the situation"[7] when
it is different from the doctor's, and how one seeks to resolve
this difference, constitutes the basis of negotiations. Whether
or not these negotiations are successful, i.e., the doctor and
patient come to some agreement about what the patient's problem
is and what to do about it, the formal features noted above are
binding. The peculiar part of all of this is that the partici-
pants to these negotiations are rarely aware of them. The
doctor's position is that his diagnosis was reached independent
of the patient's assessment, while the patient feels that they

sought out the doctor in the first place because "he knows" and
they don't, and that they (the patient) have had little if any
influence upon the doctor's "scientific" appraisal of their
condition.

Within the psychiatric interview that is a part of the family
meeting, successful negotiations are contingent upon the family
and consultant being able to communicate. This in turn is made
possible by both parties being able to accept certain sets of
common sense assumptions. While the therapist claims to be
scientific and the child and family rely on common sense, both
in fact share certain basic notions. We have outlined below
some of the consultant's "scientific" tacid understandings and
contrasted them to those of the layman.

1. One's present and future condition is contingent upon
    one's past. Common sense will buy that.
2. The individual is a product of his upbringing, i.e.,
    "if you brought them up right, they turned out right."
    The millions of copies of "How to bring up baby" books
    sold, attest to the fact that common sense will buy that
    one too.
3. How well you succeed in accomplishing Step #2 is
    contingent upon how well the family gets along, i.e., if
    family members like each other, that's good; if they
    don't, that's bad. Common sense will buy that.
4. Love is an important feature of the human condition.
    Persons who love someone who love them back are happy,
    while those who don't are not. Common sense will buy
    that.
5. In "primary relationships", honesty is the best policy,
    i.e., lying and deceit does little to build basic trust.
    Common sense will buy that.
6. Some or many of our actions are unconsciously motivated,
    i.e., sometimes we can't explain why we did what we did.
    With the proliferation of Freudian terminology and the
    public's awareness of it, at least on the level of
    "vulgar Freudianism", common sense can buy that. Indeed
    Freud is now as much a part of common sense in some
    circles, as common sense is a part of Freud.
7. If a family member has a "problem", it is seen as in
    part cause and effect, i.e., the family played some role
    in causing the problem, and is effected by it. Leaving
    alone who is to take the blame or how the family can
    repair the damage, common sense will buy that.

8. Some persons, aware of all of the above, are because
   of their training better able than others to find the
   cause and remedy for the family's problems. The fact
   that so many persons seek out psychiatrists, psychologists, and clinicians of every sort, not to mention
   the booming sales in pop psychology books, attests to
   the fact that common sense will buy that.

In fact, it may not be overstating the case to contend that
many of the basic assumptions held by the consultants in their
effort to interpret and understand the family's problems were,
or came to be accepted by the family. This, of course, occurs
only in the case of successful negotiations. In those instances
where the therapist and patient are unable to transcend mutually
antagonistic models, negotiations may end in failure. In extreme
cases of unsuccessful negotiations, the patient may be committed
to "care".

This process of negotiating reality plays itself out not only
within the family meeting, but in other contexts as well. We
will see how the consultants, acting on behalf of the Center,
seek to successfully negotiate the child's reality with the
court.

Before entering into this analysis, let us reverse our field
for a moment, and consider why in so many cases, the family
meeting was considered so essential. After all, there are other
therapists, invoking other therapies, who also seek to understand
the patient's present problem by way of his/her past, who do not
initiate family meetings, nor do they see any compelling reason
to do so. The most obvious answer to this question turns on
the fact that the consultants were not only therapists, but
family therapists. As such, they would need to see the family
as a unit in order to be able to make a diagnosis and recommendation to the court. However, there are some less obvious
reasons for these meetings as well. (1) There is the need to
gather firsthand information about the child's current problem
and the particulars of the case. (2) The family meeting helps
to legitimate to the court the assessment team's efforts on
behalf of the child and court. (3) In some cases the family
meeting is not used to gather information. In these cases the
staff have already decided what to do on the basis of the
professional meeting and available information and use the
family meeting as a forum for "selling" the parents on their
definition of the problem and what to do about it. In such
cases, the family enters the meeting unaware of this hidden
agenda. (4) The assessment team can claim (through family

meetings) to be judging each case upon its own merits, and not upon its abstract resemblance to other cases "like it".

CONSTRUCTING REPORTS

We will now go on to consider how the consultants with their "scientific" outlook, and the court and family with their lay or "common sense" perspective succeed or fail to reach some common agreement regarding the child's problems. We will do this through an analysis of the assessment team's final report to the court, which is comprised of three parts: (1) The psychiatric report, (2) The psychologist's report (based primarily upon the results of a battery of psychological tests) and (3) The "house report" of the CCOs.

These reports inform as much by what they do not say as what they do. The author's analysis will provide alternative ways of interpreting the content and show how the consultants sought to construct matters so that the court would accept their version of reality over competing versions. The text of the report is given below.

This report is based on the information I have obtained from my involvement with Joan W. and her family since September 1977 when she was transferred to the Assessment Centre from St. Mary's following the complete breakdown of her placement there. I have had five meetings with all the professional workers involved in her care, and in addition many informal discussions particularly with her social worker, Miss J.S., and her Childcare worker at Oxford, Mr. J. The assessment practice at the Centre is to see the children with their families and not individually. I have had five family meetings with Mrs. W., Joan and Sally, her twin sister together with Miss and Mr. J. on one occasion in their own home. I have arranged for Joan to be assessed psychologically by Mrs. E. (Psychologist) who saw her originally in 1974. Because of pressure of time, I am incorporating her report here. Previous Court Reports and the three to six monthly reports on Joan made by the staff at St. Mary's throughout her stay, have also been made available to me.

As the court is aware, our original intention was that I should attempt to make a therapeutic relationship with the W. (family) by means of working with them as a family, in order to alleviate the serious emotional problems,

considered by all who know them, to exist in this family.
I feel it is necessary to point out that I believe it likely
that the divulgence of the contents of this report to Joan
and her mother and the personal appearance of myself and
Mr. J. in Court may jeopardise the fragile working relationship which we now have with the W. (family). I recognize
that this may nevertheless be unavoidable. I think it is
important to point out that Mrs. W. has throughout
cooperated with our wish to see them as a family. Whilst
what has been achieved so far is very limited this is the
first time that Mrs. W. has agreed to work with a psychiatrist with her children. This may reflect, again for the
first time, a covert acknowledgement by her that the family
has some psychological problems.

The court is aware of the details of Joan's background,
but in order to understand the present situation in which
Mrs. W. is contesting the Care Order again, certain important factors should be noted.

Joan and Sally were born after the death of their father,
and Mrs. W. has been largely unsupported by family and
friends throughout their childhood. I understand that Joan
spent much of the first year of her life in hospital and
during her first five years had as many as five different
homes. For much of this time, she was not cared for
primarily by her mother. At the age of five, the girls
joined their mother in England, but were soon admitted to
St. Mary's nursery in 1970. From the records and from what
I have been told by the workers involved with the family
from that time on there does not appear to have been a time
when Mrs. W. has cared for the two girls unaided. It is
known that children whose early life history is characterised by frequent moves of home and changes of caretakers
are predisposed to psychological disturbance in later life,
and in particular to anti-social behaviour and depression.
Some of Joan's behaviour noted throughout professional
contact with her from the age of five may be attributed to
the difficult start she had. It is worth noting that since
Joan's move to Oxford Mrs. W. has been looking after Sally
at home by herself, apparently successfully. It is possible
that the intensive help given to Mrs. W. has now resulted
in an increased capacity to mother her children and may soon
mean that she is able to care for the relatively undisturbed
child that Sally appears to be. But there is an important
difference between the two girls, in that, again from the
records, it appears that Joan was less favoured by her
mother from her earliest years. Still today, Joan regards

herself as the "mad, bad twin", and her sister as the "good
twin".

Although there were times when an affectionate relationship was observed between Mrs. W. and Joan, the more usual
picture has been of an aggressive, attention seeking,
miserable child who was not obviously attached to her
mother. She, in turn, seemed largely indifferent to Joan.
As time went on, Joan became more openly defiant and aggressive towards her mother and Mrs. W.'s rejecting attitude
towards her became more obvious. For example, she would
take Sally home for weekends but not Joan. At home, in
contrast to Sally, Joan apparently carried out many household chores for her mother, and still does, presumably
partly as an attempt to please and placate her mother, a
characteristic of some rejected children. Nevertheless, it
must be said that Mrs. W. has not neglected the children's
physical needs and is generous to the point of indulgence.

At the time, however, when her junior school was unable any
longer to tolerate Joan's disturbed behaviour (e.g., throw-
ing chairs) at the age of nine years, and a recommendation
for maladjusted schooling was made; there was a shift in
Mrs. W.'s perception of Joan. From having been seen by her
mother as bad Joan has been perceived in the last two to
three years, as the victim of a destructive persecuting
world as exemplified by St. Mary's, Social Services, and
the Educational Services. Her behavioural disturbance,
whilst acknowledged by Mrs. W., is attributed solely to her
experiences in care and Mrs. W. draws the conclusion based
on this view, that Joan will only deteriorate further if
she remains in care but will be able to lead a normal life
albeit with help if she returns home.

Joan shows the extreme loyalty which children have for
their parents, particularly when there is an intensely
ambivalent relationship and hence shares publicly her
mother's persecuted view and her wish to return home. But
the fact of her great behavioural deterioration following
her mother's decision to appeal against the Care Order and
her increasingly difficult behaviour at Oxford when this
hearing was adjourned is probably evidence of her anxiety
about a return home, as well as a reflection of the effect
on her of a further period of insecurity. Joan has not
known where she was going to live permanently for the last
three years and this is a factor in her present day
disturbance.

Joan is a physically well developed, attractive, and
occasionally charming girl, of average ability, who has
despite her difficult circumstances reached the scholastic

attainments of an eleven-year-old. She is ambitious but
finds it hard to persist in the face of failure, which she
tends to attribute to external factors. She lacks confidence and her extreme restlessness means that she requires
much individual attention of the sort she is likely to find
only in a school such as chalet which she is presently
attending.

There is no evidence of formal psychiatric disorder.
Psychological testing, however, reveals a very emotionally
immature and deprived girl functioning at the level of a
six-year-old who still hopes for her early needs to be met
but tries to avoid the pain of disappointment by remaining
relatively uninvolved with the people in her environment,
distrustful and suspicious. She is miserable and angry and
there is some suggestion of the development of paranoid
traits. There is also evidence of a capacity to use help
in the form of a psychotherapeutic relationship but she
would require a relatively stable environment for this.

Her behaviour in Oxford described in Mr. J.'s report, at
school and to some extent in the family sessions bears out
the test results. When I have seen her, usually she is
rude, uncooperative, and unforthcoming. She is very rest-
less, finds it difficult to concentrate, to listen or
participate in the sessions for any length of time. She
appears to be anxious, on guard all the time and very wary
of her mother's responses. The discussions in the sessions
are very much limited by Mrs. W.'s refusal to acknowledge
the very serious nature of Joan's problems, which makes it
difficult for Joan to participate in a realistic way. But
there have been indications that Joan sees herself to some
extent as responsible for her actions. Mrs. W. fluctuates
so that on the one hand she has been supporting of the
staff's attempts consistently to contain Joan's behaviour
but on the other hand attributes its source to outside
agencies. Mrs. W. has occasionally hinted that she has
found Joan's behaviour extremely difficult.

I have the impression that Mrs. W. does not have the
resources required to provide Joan with the consistent limit
setting but caring control which she requires and which
professional staff are finding it extraordinary difficult
to provide her with in her present state.

It has become apparent in the family meetings, that for
understandable reasons there is little evidence of Mrs. W.,
Joan, and Sally functioning together as a family. There is
a limited but fairly affectionate bond between Sally and
Joan but that relationship is intensely rivalrous, with
much competition for their mother's favors. Sally sees her

sister as the "mad" one in the family and is on the whole
overtly complacent with her favoured position in relation to
her mother. Sally is apparently socially conforming. She
appears quite negative in the home. She is usually unforthcoming and sullen.

There has been little evidence of any mutual affection,
interest or respect expressed or demonstrated between
Mrs. W., Joan, and Sally. In fact, Mrs. W. has stated that
she does not believe that girls of twelve require physical
affection any longer. The relationship seems to be founded
on Mrs. W. supplying the girls with their material requests
for sweets, cigarettes, and so on and their angry response
if their wishes are frustrated. The girls show some
impatience with Mrs. W.'s persecuted attitudes at times, but
on the whole, they do not express individual opinions. The
only obvious strength in the family is their fierce loyalty
to one another in the face of authority.

In conclusion, I would respectfully suggest to the court
that in this case there is no straightforward answer to
the question as to whether there should be a Care Order or
not. It is clear that if the battle over Joan's care,
custody and control continues, her emotional development,
already seriously jeopardised, will be further impaired,
and as a consequence her behaviour is likely to deteriorate
further. Mrs. W. has indicated her intention to continue
the fight for her daughter whatever the outcome of this
case.

It is also my opinion that what Joan requires ideally is to
live in a therapeutic setting where she could obtain help
with her emotional problems, whilst maintaining some
contact with home and her mother. It seems unlikely that
this would be obtainable without a Care Order.

It is very doubtful that Joan's behaviour rooted as it is
in a long standing emotional deprivation is likely to alter
radically if she goes home, in the long term, despite
Mrs. W.'s belief and Joan's statement to that effect. It
may be that there would be an initial honeymoon period
which might last several months, but I think that eventually
the situation is likely to break down once again. Although
Mrs. W. has stated her intention to continue working with
us if Joan goes home, without a Care Order, the past
experience of Social Service with Mrs. W. makes it difficult
to rely on that intention in Joan's interest.

Analysing Reports

After the preliminary introductory paragraph, the report begins
with the consultant stating that the original intention of the
court was for the consultant to establish a "therapeutic
relationship" with the family. This same consultant told the
author during the taped interview that she (and the others)
made no attempt at therapy inasmuch as this would be impossible
to accomplish in 3-6 weeks (the time officially allotted by
the court for an assessment). Given that the report was written
in December of 1977, and the therapist's first involvement in
the case was September of 1977, the child had already been "in
care" for about 12 weeks. Could the staff have perhaps "allev-
iated the serious emotional problems (that) exist in this
family" in that period of time? Apparently not, for we are
told that Mrs. W. is contesting the court order in order to
gain legal custody of her daughter, and that the "professional
staff are finding it extraordinary difficult to provide her
(Joan) with ... the consistent, limit setting, but caring
control which she requires". Indeed the author knows from
informal talks with the staff that they consider Joan a "failure" and have given up trying.

The above characterizes the inherent dilemma faced by the
consultants and staff of the Center. On the one hand is the
contention that family therapy is important to both the child
and the staff, and that it should be an integral part of the
assessment process. On the other is the belief that while more
time was needed to do family therapy, the children were already
kept longer than was in their best interest.

Leaving this dilemma unresolved, we go on to consider the
question of Joan's "serious emotional problem". This too is
peculiar in that we learn later in the report that "there is
no evidence of formal psychiatric disorder".

Continuing on in paragraph two, the consultant notes that for
the court to divulge the contents of the report to the parents
or child would "jeopardize the fragile working relationship
(the staff) now have with the family". Doubtless this is true;
however, not to divulge its contents would also mean that the
charges against Mrs. W. by the agency would remain unknown to
her at a time when she is legally contesting the Center's Care
Order. We have noted in an earlier chapter the unequal balance
of power confronting the parents of children in care in their
effort to regain custody of their child. The above is a
specific instance of the general case.

Finally, we are told that Mrs. W.'s agreeing to work with a
psychiatrist for the first time "... may reflect a covert
acknowledgement by her that the family has some psychological
problems". Maybe so, but it may also reflect the fact that she
is trying to oblige the judge by "cooperating" inasmuch as she
is in the midst of a legal battle to regain the custody of her
child for the first time as well. This is not to mention the
fact that Mrs. W. and Joan have steadfastly maintained that
there were no psychological problems.

To summarize, the consultant in the second paragraph, attempts
to establish for the court the existence of emotional problems
in the family and the need for a therapeutic relationship over
and above the family's contentions to the contrary.

The third paragraph in the report picks up this theme, and
outlines for the magistrate background material from Joan's
case. This, given the consultant's psychoanalytic orientation
establishes the existence of Joan's emotional problems and their
causes, and lends support to the consultant's appraisal. It
does so while (and by) discrediting the contentions of Mrs. W.
that she is a fit mother, that it is in Joan's best interest to
return home, and that Joan's "problems" do not result from her
familial relationships, but from her institutional ones. The
report states, "Joan spent much of the first year of her life
in hospital and during her first five years had as many as five
different homes", and that "for much of this time she was not
cared for primarily by her mother". Furthermore, Joan and her
sister were committed to a children's home from 1970 to 1977,
and "there does not appear to have been a time when Mrs. W. has
cared for the two girls unaided". Allowing this, and the further
psychoanalytic contention (noted in the report) that "... Children whose early life history is characterised by frequent moves
of home and changes of caretakers are predisposed to psychological disturbance in later life and in particular to anti-
social behavior and depression" (she might have included
suicide), and we see how the consultant has in one paragraph,
discredited the mother, given support for her own assessment,
and established Joan's "serious problems". Every effort is made
in this manoeuver to "cover the rear" as it were. After all,
Joan's twin sister also experienced a broken home, institutional-
ization, and many of the other untoward events that Joan had,
and she seems "relatively undisturbed". This is dealt with by
noting that the twin was favored by the mother. If true, this
and not the list of particulars noted above, may be responsible
for Joan's "disturbance". The notion that broken homes or

other forms of "early childhood trauma" *per se*, predispose to
depression and/or suicide in later life has been disputed elsewhere by the author.[8]

Paragraph four goes on to characterize Joan in the family
therapy interview as "aggressive, attention seeking, miserable
child who was not obviously attached to her mother. She, in
turn, seems largely indifferent to Joan." This observation is
designed to strengthen the consultant's position regarding the
existence of family problems. However, one can only wonder why,
if the mother is indifferent to her daughter, she is engaged
in a legal battle to contest the Care Order, and return her
daughter to her home. While it was true that Joan is "aggressive, abusive, attention seeking, and frequently miserable", and
"not obviously attached to her mother", it was just as obvious
that she was that way at Oxford as well, and that she was not
attached to the staff, or for that matter, they to her. Given
the above, where would her "best interests" lie?

This question is especially telling when we read that when Joan
is in her mother's home she "... apparently carried out many
household chores for her mother, and still does". This is
interpreted by the consultant (given her orientation) as
"presumably partly an attempt to please and placate her
mother, a characteristic of some rejected children". Maybe so,
but she rarely volunteered at Oxford to do chores in order to
placate the staff. We have previously noted that while the
staff worked to make the house a "home", the children rarely
saw it that way and why. In fact, it may be argued that Joan
helped her mother because she was attached to her, and that the
above gesture indicated this in some "obvious way". That the
mother was also "attached" was indicated (apart from her legal
battle) by the fact noted in the report that "... Mrs. W. has
not neglected the children's physical needs and is generous to
the point of indulgence".

There follows next Mrs. W.'s contention (within the last 3 years)
that Joan's behavioural problems stem not from her familial
associations but her having become "... the victim of a destructive persecuting world as exemplified by St. Mary's (the Children's home) Social Services, and the Educational Services".
Mrs. W. further believes that "Joan will only deteriorate further
if she remains in care, but will be able to lead a normal life,
albeit with help, if she returns home." What's more, Joan
believes as her mother does.

This contention is discredited by the consultant in the following fashion. First, upon hearing of her mother's intention to
contest the Care Order, Joan exhibited "behavioral deterioration"
at Oxford, "... probably evidence of her anxiety about a return
home, as well as a reflection of the effect on her of further
period of insecurity". This "behavioral deterioration", the
author feels needs to be put in context. Joan's behavior while
at Oxford was according to staff, never anything "to write home
about". She was always loud, abusive, aggressive, and indifferent to house rules. Indeed, she stood out in that regard. To
say that her behavior deteriorated upon hearing of her mother's
custody battle, is no indication that it had deteriorated from
some normal state, i.e., that Joan was happy and/or well
adjusted at Oxford, and unhappy to learn she might have to
return home to her mother. Indeed, we have already been told
that in many regards, she behaved more appropriately at home.
There is also the real possibility that her "deteriorating
behavior" was a function of her relationship to the Center's
staff, and not her "anxiety" about returning home. In fact, it
would come as no surprise to the author to find that Joan was
in a constant state of "anxiety", given the fact that she
"... has not known where she was going to live permanently for
the last three years", and that she had not lived anywhere
permanently prior to that.

In summary, we find in paragraph four that both the consultant
and mother believe that Joan's behavioral problems stem from
the past. The difference was this. The consultant, because of
her Freudian orientation, tries to establish Joan's problem in
"broken homes", "early childhood trauma", and "maternal
deprivation".[9] This would locate the cause of the problem in
the "family dynamics". Mrs. W. chose another piece of Joan's
biography to focus on, the last 3 years (the consultant
focused on the first 3). This would locate the blame not in
the family, but in the institutional care Joan received. Given
their different "purpose at hand", their different allocations
of blame are in no way surprising.

Paragraph five of the report opens with the observation that
"there is no evidence of formal psychiatric disorder", but then
goes on to state that psychological testing suggests "the
development of paranoid traits". The psychological profile is
one of a girl who ... "tries to avoid the pain of disappointment
by remaining relatively uninvolved with people in her environment, distrustful, and suspicious". Given her past experiences
and current environment, can this be viewed as mal-adaptive?

The paragraph ends with the notation "there is also evidence of
a capacity to use help in the form of a psychotherapeutic
relationship but she would require a relatively stable environment". Given the fact that by the time the study was over,
Joan had been at Oxford for 12 months and shown no signs of
improvement, one can only conclude: (a) Oxford could not
provide a "psychotherapeutic relationship", (b) Oxford does not
provide a "relatively stable environment" or, (c) Psychotherapeutic relationships take longer than 12 months to establish.

Paragraph six is really an extension of the topic treated in
paragraph five. Here, Mrs. W. acknowledges that Joan has
behavioral problems (is sometimes difficult), but does not
acknowledge the existence of psychological problems. She
attributes Joan's misbehavior to outside agencies, while the
consultant sees them as symptomatic of psychological problems
caused by family dynamics.

Paragraph seven cautions the court that Mrs. W. probably "does
not have the resources required to provide Joan with the
consistent, limit setting but caring control which she
requires". Of course, the latter part of the same sentence
indicates (in a badly understated way) that the staff cannot
provide these resources either. We will see how this hedging
strategy provides a basis for the conclusions forthcoming in
paragraph nine. First, let's look at paragraph eight.

This section of the report opens with a reiteration of the fact
that there seems to be little overt mutual affection between
Mrs. W. and her daughter. The fact that as much could be said
for the overt mutual affection demonstrated between Joan and
the staff, is conspicuously absent. The report goes on to
note that Mrs. W. "... does not believe that girls of twelve
require physical affection any longer". The report fails to
note that if the staff at Oxford think girls of twelve require
physical affection they rarely demonstrated it. In short, if
Mrs. W. does not show Joan physical affection from conviction,
the staff did not show it either, for whatever reason. I
suspect both failed in this regard for the same reason, i.e.,
Joan was not a "loving child". She was abusive, "uncooperative
and unforthcoming". It is not only very difficult to generate
feelings of affection for a child of this sort, but even if one
managed it, it is extremely difficult to display them without
untoward consequences. Joan was as likely to meet a kindness
with a "piss off" as a "thank you".

The report continues by noting that the mother's "... relationship seems to be founded on ... supplying the girls with their
material requests for sweets, cigarettes, and so on ...". This
comment is included not only to describe the nature of the
relationship between Mrs. W. and her daughters, but, as noted
in an earlier chapter, to indicate the staff's displeasure with
parent's "bribing" their children, and how these "bribes" serve
to undo what good the staff has managed to accomplish at the
Center. However, this may be read in another way, that is, as
an indication of Mrs. W.'s attachment to her child. The staff,
for its part, preferred viewing these efforts as stemming less
from generosity than guilt.

The final line notes that "the only obvious strength in the
family is their fierce loyalty to one another in the face of
authority". In terms of "family dynamics", this is indeed a
significant strength and perhaps a key one in keeping the
family together. After all, Joan and her mother have spent
a lifetime dealing with authority from a disadvantaged position.
That the family gains some strength in this undertaking from a
"fierce loyalty" ought to be seen as a big plus. Clearly, the
staff viewed it otherwise, and depending upon the context,
sometimes saw such "anti-authoritarian tendencies" as stemming
from "paranoid tendencies". Lemert has shown how the organizational attribution of paranoid tendencies often results in a
self-fulfilling prophecy. As such, they may be not only mis-
leading, but therapeutically counter-productive.[10]

This leads us to paragraph nine and the beginning of the
"conclusions". As noted in our discussion of paragraph seven,
the strategy of hedging bets on what was in the child's best
interest was a prelude of things to come. For example, this
section opens with "in conclusion, I would respectfully suggest
to the court that in this case there is no straightforward
answer to the question as to whether there should be a Care
Order or not." This would seem an honest and straightforward
appraisal on the part of the consultant. Given the preceding
discussion, we have seen that there was good ground for
questioning what was "in the best interest of the child".

However, this was not the consultant's "bottom line", and the
initial ambiguity is resolved in the following fashion in favor
of a "Care Order". First the blame was put squarely back upon
Mrs. W. "It is clear that if the battle over Joan's care,
custody, and control continues, her emotional development,
already seriously jeopardized, will be further impaired, and as

consequence, her behavior is likely to deteriorate further.
Mrs. W. has indicated her intention to continue the fight for
her daughter whatever the outcome of this case." Clearly, from
the consultant's perspective, Mrs. W. is not acting in her
child's best interest. At this point, the consultant strengthens
her position by recommending what she thinks would be in the
child's best interest, "it is my opinion that what Joan requires
ideally is to live in a therapeutic setting where she could
obtain help with her emotional problems, whilst maintaining
some contact with home and her mother. It seems unlikely that
this would be accomplished without a Care Order".

What is conspicuously absent from the report is a fact that
the consultant and staff were both well aware of, that achieving
this ideal situation would be just as unlikely with a Care
Order. In fact, therapeutic settings were unavailable, now or
in the foreseeable future. This left the child with one of two
"real options", i.e., to remain at Oxford (where she has already
spent 12 months) for some indefinite period of time until a
therapeutic setting becomes available, or be moved out of
Oxford into a "long-term care facility" of some sort, at least
on a "holding basis". It is clear that these options were not
ideal either. In fact, there are good grounds for supposing
that, given the alternatives, returning the child to her mother
was not a bad idea.

This possibility is discredited by the consultant in the last
paragraph. It also effectively resolves the ambiguity about
what to do with Joan found in the beginning of paragraph nine.
The consultant's position is given the force of authority
through the list of credentials following her signature at the
end of the report: M.B., B.S., D.Obst., R.C.O.G., D.P.M.,
M.R.C. Psych., consultant psychiatrist. If the consultant's
contention is true that "It is very doubtful that Joan's
behavior rooted as it is in long standing emotional deprivation
is likely to alter radically if she goes home", it is equally
true that it is unlikely to alter radically for the better if
she remains at Oxford. Mrs. W. and the staff were both convinced that 12 months there has done little to improve Joan's
disposition. Furthermore, recognizing that the staff has
"given up on Joan", there is little reason to suppose that
matters would improve with time.

Quite apart from what was in Joan's best interest, was the
staff's off-the-record concern for what was in the best interest
of the other children. Joan's disruptive influence upon the
Center has made it extremely difficult for them to work with

the other children. Given all of this, one might have expected
that the assessment team, headed by the psychiatric consultant,
would have recommended to the court that the care order be
rescinded and the mother be given custody of the child. We have
seen that such was not the case. Part of the reason for this
can be accounted for by the consultant's professional orientation to which facts in the case were important and how they
were to be interpreted. Add to this, the staff's contention
that "when in doubt, believe the consultant", and we can see
how and why "a consensus" was reached, and the report took the
form it did. However, this is only a partial accounting. For
a more complete understanding of how the assessment team reached
its decision, we will need to consider the last stage of the
assessment process, the case conference. It was on the basis of
this meeting that the final recommendation to the court was
formulated.

                    THE CASE CONFERENCE

As previously indicated, the final case conference came after
the professional and family meetings, and served as a platform
for airing differences and sifting information. Present at
these meetings were all professional persons involved in any
way with the case, e.g., the RCCOs the consultant (who chaired
the meeting), senior staff, teachers, and the field social
worker. All in all, a dozen persons might attend the final
staff meeting. Each of these professionals had prepared a
report, and everyone was to be heard from. Following the
presentations, (or during it) the floor was open to debate.
Issues in the case were discussed and differences of opinion
aired. This was to be the case's final resting place and the
forum in which some consensus would be reached upon what was
"in the best interest of the child". These reports were based
upon weeks or months of observations and preparation, and were
to culminate in a final synthesis — a recommendation to the
court.

How long did this process take? One and a half hours to be
exact, the time any one consultant chairing the meeting gave to
the Center per week. How could twelve people present, consider,
debate, and conclude a discussion of this magnitude in
90 minutes? The answer is the punch line to the oldest joke
in the world, "with great effort". Given the fact that all
meetings were given to late starts, and that the discussion and
negotiation period exceeded the time given to formal presentations, each contributor had about 3 or 4 minutes in which to

offer and defend their findings. How was this managed? It
wasn't. Many people did not contribute. Residential childcare
officers, for example, typically said little or nothing.

How could those in attendance make a rational decision on behalf
of the child if they could not present and weigh all of the
relevant information? Easy. The staff meetings, while officially given as the place where final decisions on the assessment
were made, were not utilized in this way. Most persons entering
the staff meeting had already made up their mind about what was
in the child's best interest and why, through informal discussions in the kitchen, or over a drink after work. One might
protest that they had not heard all relevant information bearing
upon the case. No matter, they had heard enough, either by
reviewing the records, their own observations of the child and
parent, or by way of informal conversations with relevant third
parties. It was upon this informal network of information and
influence that decisions were made, and not upon the rational
con·ideration of professional reports formally presented in
staff meetings. "Consensus" was also, to a large extent, the
result of these outside informal negotiations.

What of the final recommendation? What happened after deciding
through informal channels what was in the best interest of the
child, and using the staff meetings as a way to formalize and
legitimate these decisions to the court. The process went
something like this. First there was an effort to get consensus
upon which of the many theoretical alternatives open to the
child would be in his best interest. Having decided what was
theoretically best, the placement officer was consulted to see
what was realistically available. The goodness of fit between
the former and the latter were usually very poor. Apart from
the question of whether or not the assessment team was able to
rationally decide what was in the child's best interest (we
have already offered some basis for skepticism, more will
follow in Chapter 6) the fact was that the real available
choices usually bore little if any resemblance to the ideal
recommendation. In fact, the recommendation to the court was
rarely what the assessment team felt was "in the child's best
interest". Rather, the staff worked to get the child the
least bad "real" available option. Sometimes the court was
made privy to this dilemma, other times it was not. While the
consultants and staff felt that the courts needed educating in
these matters, they did not view themselves as social reformers,
but as therapists, and as such, were not prepared, either with
time or effort, to undertake the court's education.

We have dealt in this chapter with the assessment process, who participated in it, why it took the form it did, and its immediate outcome for the court and child. Let us now consider the impending move to the new facility, its architectural characteristics, and its real and potential effects upon the staff and children.

5

The New Facility: The Dark Before the Storm

We have already seen how the staff were anxious on many fronts about the impending move to the new facility. What was it that provoked all this anxiety? Thus far, we have noted the unknown qualities of the new superintendent, the competition for promotions, the fate of family therapy, Alec's role in the newly structured hierarchy, whether or not the two houses reconstituted under one roof would be able to sustain their former identities, how institutionalized the agency would become in the new setting, and how one could ever hope to establish a home in a "house" like Queen's Road.

Many of these organizational concerns turned directly upon the design of the new building. We will now deal with some of these features, and how they worked to engender a feeling of uneasiness among the staff.

DESIGN "FEATURES"

First and foremost it is the task of the CCO to provide for the safety and well being of the child. Such an undertaking required a lot of effort at Oxford and Cambridge. The teams in both houses were usually understaffed and overworked. The same staff was now expected to care for the same number of children under one roof. All things being equal, one might expect the task to have been lightened under these circumstances. No one among the staff held this view. To begin with, here as in most social situations, all things were not equal. One consultant to the Center expressed his concern in a mimeographed "Discussion Document". The following is an excerpt from that report.

"Residential care for children is threatened with a poten-
tially rapidly deteriorating situation, both in reducing
quality of care and escalating costs. The main aim of this
paper however is to point out that the present situation
presents a unique opportunity to *improve* care for much *less*
money than is otherwise likely. What is required is a
different approach to assessment. Instead of bringing
children to a large centralised observation and assessment
centre (Queen's Road) the assessment team could go to the
child — either in his home or in a small local children's
home if he has to come into care. The assessment could
then work with the children's home to facilitate a return
home or to help establish a prolonged stay at that home,
depending on how the situation develops. Some children
would move on to fostering/adoption and a few to specialised
children's homes.
   This arrangement would stop the first experience of *all*
children coming into care being that of a short term
'bridging stay' in an institution, a situation which sets
a trend towards further breakdown of placements and insti-
tutionalization of children.
   (Queen's Road) is impressive but totally unsuitable for
either young or disturbed children. All visits by childcare specialists verify this. The views of the staff of
the Assessment Centre have been given to various members of
residential management and Social Services Committee over
the last two or three years. Details of the dangers,
physical and emotional, are detailed in the Appendix. In
summary, children's lives will be at risk and the social
organization that the building will impose on staff and
children will make for greater difficulties in control but
at the same time a greater need for that control. More
staff will be needed inside the building and less work can
be done on returning children to their home. The result
will be a higher percentage of children going onto long
stay homes, and, because highly disturbed children will not
be contained, we will also have to use regional assessment
centers more — we are now one of the lowest users. This
will be very expensive and bad childcare.

From the staff's point of view, one key feature of being able
to provide for the safety and wellbeing of children in institutional settings is containment. There were two doors in
Oxford and Cambridge. There were literally dozens of exits in
the building at Queen's Road. "Keeping an eye" on sixteen
children under such circumstances would be nearly impossible.
One remedy would be to lock some of the exits. However, this
would have been contrary to existing fire codes.

In addition to the number of doors opening to the outside, was
the endless number of doors, stairways, and cubicles inside the
building where children could be "out of sight and out of mind".
In fact, the innards were such a maze that a social service
employee who had shown visitors through the building innumerable
times became hopelessly lost while giving the author a guided
tour.

Apart from the number of doors, there was a problem with their
width. Most inside doors were very narrow. The acting superintendent, a portly woman, literally went through doorways side-
ways. Many CCOs questioned whether the door dimensions were up
to building code. If so, it was their opinion there was something wrong with the code.

Leaving alone the number of doors and their size, there was the
question of where they led. Many led to the roof which contained
(not by design) a veritable jungle-gym and natural playground
for bored children seeking adventure. As such, it also held
innumerable hazards, none of which the staff felt it would be
able to monitor.

Windows were also potential hazards. Inasmuch as Queen's Road
was a "modern facility", it was built in the modern mode, i.e.,
the windows in the children's bedrooms (and on most outer walls)
were floor to ceiling. Keeping in mind that it was not unusual
at Oxford and Cambridge for the children to break windows,
windows of the sort found at Queen's Road were a threat to life
and limb. There was the added worry among staff that if a
window should be broken, the child could easily fall out. This
led to yet another concern about where they would fall. All of
the children's bedrooms were strung in a row (motel style)
along the outer wall facing the front of the building on the
second floor. Beneath them was a large concrete courtyard. A
child falling onto this area would almost certainly sustain
serious injury.

Another feature of the building the staff did not appreciate
was the elimination of the kitchen which had always been the
center of social life for both staff and children. There was,
of course, a food preparation facility in the new building, but
this was an efficient open area designed for cooking, not
socializing. Also included were separate dining facilities for
the staff and children. This, too, was an unwelcome "plus" in
that it was considered an important feature at Oxford and
Cambridge that children and staff dined together. Communal
meals were seen by the staff as an essential part of their

effort on behalf of the children to make a home within the
house.

Another bigger but not better feature was the sheer size of the
place which offered much more space than either the staff or
children required. In conjunction with the vastness, was the
fact that the building had no elevators. This meant not only
more work for the staff, but also excluded the possibility of
caring for disabled children. One worker expressed his concern
in this way.

> "I'm worried that it's going to, as far as I can see, going
> to change the ambiance of the place because of the physical
> properties of the building where we're going (the new
> facility) we are going to need to be more controlling of
> the children, in terms of keeping them enclosed in a space,
> which is a step backwards (in care).
> It's a very mazey, strange place, which is full of physical
> dangers to small children and disturbed children — lots of
> easy suicide leaps, which is going to make us more contain-
> ing, I think. It's very big and spacious, and it's
> strangely built. It's got very narrow corridors with low
> ceilings, and the door openings are so narrow that they
> could only buy knock-down furniture."

Another had this to say:

> "It's much easier to get the feel of anxiety once you've
> actually seen the place (the new facility). As I say, it's
> hard to put into words, but the first time I went there I
> think everybody else is affected in much the same way, that
> you're completely taken aback by it all. It's very hard to
> take it all in, and you're almost speechless. Exasperated.
> And I think everybody came away after the first visit feel-
> ing very depressed about it."

Quite apart from the question of the rational organization of
inner space, there was the outer appearance of the building.
As the staff viewed it, this can best be summarized by one
word — "ominous". The building was constructed of concrete
bricks, and notwithstanding the generous use of glass, looked
like a fortification or "blockhouse". The look was definitely
"institutional".

Queen's Road was also an integral part of Council Housing. At
the time of my tour, it had the following appearance as viewed
from the roof. On one side was Council Housing surrealistically

stretching off the horizon, and on the other side the rubble
of buildings a part of urban renewal. To the rear of the
facility was the railroad track, and in front more construction.
A patch of green was nowhere in sight. In short, from an
aesthetic point of view, the new facility and its setting left
much to be desired.

In all fairness, the entire "estate" was still under construction. The diagram below gives the reader a better idea of
where the assessment center was situated within the complex, and
indicates the future coming of a large public park, youth club
and play center. The author does not know when these facilities
will be completed, or if the children at the center were meant
to share in them. At no point did the staff refer to these
facilities or indicate that they were intended to become a part
of the assessment center.

Other features of the building were ill conceived, and would
make things more difficult for the childcare officers. For
example, the tiled bathtubs were molded into the concrete floor
below floor level. While aesthetically pleasing, they made the
routine task of bathing the smaller children almost impossible.
The workers would almost certainly have to enter the tub themselves to bathe the children. These and other design problems
were pointed out to Social Services and the Housing Council.
Some were rectified before the move, others were not.

The reader should bear in mind that the move to the new facility
was scheduled 2 years before the actual move was made. In the
interim, the design and location of the building was the topic
of heated discussion among the staff and the cause of great
anxiety. This says nothing of the fact that the building was
10 years in materializing, and that during that time, the
philosophy of childcare had radically changed. What once might
have passed for a reasonable or even forward looking solution
to reception and assessment centers, was, by the time of its
completion, recognized by the staff, consultants, and the new
superintendent, as a bad mistake.

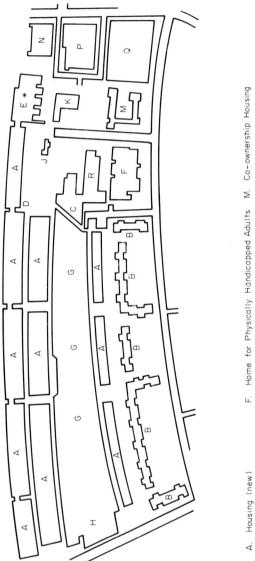

A. Housing (new)

B. Housing (existing)

C. Tenants' Hall

D. Shops

*E. Children's Reception Home

F. Home for Physically Handicapped Adults

G. Public Park

H. Play Centre

J. Youth Club

K. Housing for Elderly People

M. Co-ownership Housing

N. Shops, Studios

P. Housing and Workshops

Q. Site for Housing

R. School for Handicapped Children

NEGATIVE EFFECTS

How did the above effect the prospects for childcare at the new
facility? The answer to this question took many forms. Some
CCOs felt that the problem of containment would be met by
radical measures, e.g., locking the children in or out of their
rooms in order to limit their space. This would be, according
to many, the natural consequence and end result of the self-
fulfilling prophecy of an "institutional looking building"
functioning in an institutional way. Others felt that inasmuch
as there was no realistic way of transforming this "house" into
a home, any attempts at family therapy within the new setting
would be futile and many anticipated its quick demise.

The overall effect of the move would be to change the assessment
center, as the staff had known it, from a "homey" to a
"custodial" environment. They also imagined the counterpart to
custodial care, i.e., more structure and rules, not just for
the children, but for the workers. This they equated with a
less meaningful form of care, and consequently with less
meaningful work. In this regard, many anticipated a large turnover in personnel in an otherwise stable workforce. As
previously indicated, some had applied for jobs elsewhere,
"just in case". In keeping with this anticipated transformation
to a custodial setting, was the new superintendent, who you will
remember came from "probation" and was, based upon the staff's
first impressions, an "organizational man". Add to these problems those discussed earlier in the chapter, and one has an
impressive list of divisive effects upon the agency and staff
that are a direct result of the impending move.

POSITIVE EFFECTS

Having considered how the new facility and the move to it
resulted in what the staff felt would be the reorganization of
the existing agency, a new orientation to childcare, antagonisms
within the staff, low morale, and the demise of family therapy,
let us now consider what a minority of staff hoped would become
a change for the better.

First and foremost in this search for optimism was the new
superintendent. While his first impression on staff was generally poor because of his dress, demeanor, and a number of minor
but unpopular in-house directives (which he later withdrew or
ignored), Digby was, with time, seen by some as a fair and
reasonable person. Given the staff's view of the acting

superintendent, this was a step up. While Digby's administrative skills were unknown, Sylvia's were considered mediocre at best. This too provided hope. Finally, there was the covert feeling among some of the staff (nearly all of whom were women) that a male superintendent was preferable. This was true not because men were considered better administrators. Rather, a male superintendent was seen as a way of forestalling romantic rivalries and jealousies that developed among women CCOs toward male workers. These problems when they occurred, were not only personal, but had political and economic repercussions as well.

In addition to the new superintendent, there was Alec's role under the reorganization plan. It was hoped that he would have the same, or nearly the same status within the agency that Sylvia had, and that this new-found strength would enable him to act more effectively both as a buffer between Sylvia and the other staff, and as an effective liaison to Digby.

If some of the staff were disgruntled as a result of the reorganization, others were pleased. After all, the winners in the competition for promotions gained an increase in status and pay. However, even here some qualification is required. Some who were promoted in rank, for example Sylvia and Judy, actually suffered a net loss in pay. This resulted from their loss of "acting" status. As "acting superintendent" and "acting head of home", Sylvia and Judy made more money before the reorganization than after. This was for both (but especially Sylvia) insult to injury.

Commuting was another consideration. Depending upon where one lived, some found the location of the new facility easier to reach while others found it less convenient. The former considered the easier access a small fringe benefit.

Finally, some staff viewed the move in a sort of negative-positivistic way. By this I have two things in mind. First, while all staff disliked the new facility, and many expected to resign soon after their arrival, the move provided some with an increase in status and pay, and a boost up the Social Service career ladder. Inasmuch as promotions within the agency were in no way guaranteed, and were few and far between, the move to the new facility and the reorganization it necessitated, was seen by those benefiting from it as a boon. Secondly, some staff felt that nothing positive could happen during the transition or "holding period" and that there was at least hope when the move was completed.

"I started off saying I'm not going to work there (Queen's
Road), but I'm gonna be there until something else crops up
(he will leave at the first opportunity). But as long as
I'm still here, I don't think it's any use to anybody to
sort of keep thinking, oh Christ, what's going to happen?
We're not going to get anywhere (doing that). We have to
sort of get ourselves together and say, right, it's a
shitty place, but we're going to make the best of it cause
that's where we're going.... And just get things rolling
(more staff-child and staff-staff interaction groups going).
Otherwise, the whole thing is just going to fall to
bits.... I don't know how other people feel about it, (the
move) I know a lot of people feel anxious about the place,
I do, but I think that we've really got to think positive,
you know, rather than negative. Otherwise, it's going to
be a shit. We're not going to get anywhere."

Having covered in the first five chapters a description of the
reception and assessment center, who worked there, what they
did, how they got there, the nature of staff interactions, and
the ubiquitous effects of Queen's Road, we will move on to a
consideration of what all of this meant to childcare.

6

Assessing the
Assessment Center

Steven Marcus, in an essay on English history, the rise of the welfare state and its effects upon dependent persons, writes:

> "Caring for people in a concerted effort and not caring for them in a concerted effort are each of them, as matters of policy, interventions. All interventions have consequences, and one of the things we should learn to keep in the forefront of our consciousness is that most important consequences of any intervention almost always turn out to be those consequences that were not intended or planned upon or could not have been calculated beforehand. Dependents, precisely because they are dependent are often unable to help themselves, deserve more than others to be protected from the unintended consequences of our benevolence, and the incalculable consequences of our social goodwill."[1]*

CHILDCARE: FOR WEAL OR WOE?

The above is an apt sentiment for the children and parents who became involved in one way or another with the assessment center. We have in different contexts throughout the book already assessed various practices of the Center and their relationship to care.

For example, we discussed the CCOs' lack of formal on-the-job training, prior credentials, or experience; the benefits of family therapy for the clients and staff, and its diminishing presence at the center; the inequitable distribution of cases

---

*Superscript numbers refer to Notes at end of book.

among staff; the low staff morale resulting from all of the
above; the arbitrary use of power by senior staff; the ensuing
lack of basic trust on the part of junior staff; the unequal
distribution of power between the parent and assessment center
and its potential effects upon the child; the demoralizing
effect of the impending move to the new care facility; and the
nature of child-staff interaction and their effects upon the
prospects of making "a home" within "the house".

We have discussed in Chapter 4 the inner working of the assessment process, and how it is better characterized by "play it by
ear" procedures than some careful, objective, scientific
appraisal of the child's current needs and available options.
That is not to say that the staff and consultants intentionally
conspired against the child or family, or that when there were
"hidden agendas", they were not altruistically motivated. The
author was always convinced of the good intentions of the staff.
However, the assessment process, the staff's lack of formal
training, the availability of real options, time constraints,
political contingencies, low morale, and junior-senior staff
antagonisms all worked against their acting in the best interest
of the child.

The key question presents itself, notwithstanding all of these
constraining circumstances, how well did they succeed? The
peculiar fact is, no one knows. While the staff was unaware
that a problem existed, and consequently was not overly concerned about it, the consulting psychologist (who was more
research oriented) was concerned. After all, if no one knew
the consequences for the child of the staff's recommendation to
the court, how could they ever know whether or not they had
acted "in the child's best interest"? As things now stood,
they could not. The lack of longitudinal studies precluded
the staff or consultants making even "intelligent guesses",
inasmuch as there was no way to tell what had become of these
children or others in similar circumstances. Not only were the
Center's staff completely unaware of the consequences of their
actions regarding the child, but the court who had the last
word in accepting or rejecting the Center's recommendations,
had no basis in past experience for knowing whether or not it
had acted in the child's best interest either.

In fact, the psychologist was so concerned with this issue that
he undertook on his own initiative to study the question, and
sent a brief questionnaire to the heads of home where children
had been placed in care, in order to check upon their progress.
By the psychologist's own admission, the questionnaire was ill-

conceived, the response rate poor, and the answers to the
questions by the heads of home were less than heartening. In
short, this effort to assess the wisdom of the assessment team's
recommendations and the court's wisdom in following or rejecting
it, was unsuccessful. The matter, like so many others, "died
in meeting", and was never revived again.

Not only was there no information on what became of the children,
but there was none regarding the Center's "success rate". By
success rate, we mean how many children seen by the Center for
assessment were returned to their natural families. This was
the avowed goal of the Center, at least insofar as reuniting
the child with his family was seen to be consistent with his
"best interests". I was told by junior and senior staff and
the consultants that the secretary would "know about that".
Upon numerous inquiries, it turned out the secretary did not
know, and in fact, no one knew. If pressed by the author to
venture a guess, there was a fantastic range of figures given
by members of staff. The acting superintendent offering a
"success rate" for the past year that was five times higher
than that offered by a junior staff member. The fact was that
either no one knew, or no one was saying. Indeed, most staff
were guarded and/or indignant that anyone would want to know.
After all, what difference did it make? Everyone did the best
they could, and the existence of statistics would not change
matters for either the staff or children.

The fact is, of course, it does matter; for without such
information, there were no grounds for assessing the assessment
center and the accuracy of their assessments and its effect
upon the children. Not only did no one know what became of
the children after they left the Center, or whether or not the
assessment team and/or court had in fact acted in the child's
best interest, but no one had any basis for assessing whether
the initiation of "family therapy" had improved the success
rate. While it was clear that the staff benefited from family
therapy being a part of the assessment process, there was no
information (apart from antidotal material by the staff) to
decide whether or not the children had.

There were other untoward consequences to this lack of feedback
regarding the efforts of CCOs. The only source of follow-up
data the staff received on the future status of their wards
came not from Social Services, but from the daily newspaper.
Occasionally, the future lives of these children were partially
revealed in newspaper accounts of some illegal act and their
conviction by the courts. In fact, the only feedback the staff

received on the consequences of their decisions was negative
feedback; and this took its toll in contributing to the staff's
low morale, and the "second thoughts" these stories provoked in
staff about their attempts at doing good. The irony was that
from the staff's perspective, the only thing worse than not
knowing what was going on, was finding out through the effort
of outsiders, especially social scientists. As indicated
earlier, social science research (and researchers) were universally held in low esteem.

With this in mind, the reader might wonder what basis the author
has for assessing the success or failure of the Center to act on
the child's behalf? The fact is, of course, we have none, nor
has anyone else. It need hardly be pointed out that this is an
unfortunate state of affairs. As noted earlier, the dependent
"... often unable to help themselves, deserve more than others
to be protected from the consequences of our benevolence and
the incalculable consequences of our social goodwill".

While unable to provide a ready answer to the key question of
outcomes for the child, we have dealt in some detail with the
assessment center's procedures, morale, relationships with child
and family, staff-staff interactions, and a number of other
topics that bare upon the existing quality of care. We have
seen that trying to do good does not always result in good being
done. In many cases the analysis reveals not only that this is
so, but why.

RECOMMENDATIONS FOR IMPROVEMENTS

To improve upon the current state of affairs, we feel that the
following changes in policy and program would go a long way
toward lifting staff morale and with it the level of childcare
at the Center: establish a feeling of basic trust between
junior and senior staff; improve the quality of formal on-the-
job training; expand the use of family therapy and actively involve the staff in the therapeutic process; provide greater opportunity for the staff to acquire subsidized access to advanced
degree programs in social work; put residential social work on
a par with field social work in terms of status, salary, and
work week; increase the staff-to-child ratio in order to provide
the opportunity for better care and the elimination of "long
shifts"; and provide more consulting time and use this time to
better advantage. We would further recommend against the move
to the new facility, but this would be academic, since the move
has already taken place. Given the staff's feeling about the

new center, we can only recommend that Social Services work to
initiate as many of the above recommendations as they are able
and as soon as possible.

A CALL FOR ACTION

The reader may wonder if this urgency is perhaps only misplaced
pessimism. After all, things may have worked out better than
anyone had anticipated. Letters from one of the consultants
and a member of staff seem to indicate otherwise. The fact is
their worst fears were realized. Excerpts from the consultant's
letter are given below, followed by those of the childcare
officer.

> Dear Jerry:
>   I am feeling very bad about not either replying to your
> letter or doing as I said I would, that is, making a tape.
> We have been so hectic with so many differing problems that
> issues which are not of an immediate importance tend to be
> pushed to one side. I know that this is a shame because of
> the good work that you put in.
>   Briefly, things were very difficult to begin with and all
> the fears about management of the children seemed to be
> confirmed. It was difficult to contain any of the children
> in any satisfactory way and a number had to be transferred
> to other institutions. It was also interesting that a
> number of the children appeared to be heading for psychiatric
> care rather than other forms of residential care. It is
> difficult to know whether the building or the set-up was
> driving them crazy or whether this was the way that the
> staff were trying to use the psychiatrists to get rid of
> difficult children. The staff attempted to set up two
> separate units thus replicating the two previous assessment
> homes, but found it was impossible because of the building.
> They then reorganized themselves into one unit but kept the
> smaller divisions. The place has now settled down somewhat,
> and they find they can manage eight children. It is very
> unsure as to whether they can manage more however. The
> plan is to see if they can manage up to fourteen. In other
> words, they still have the same volume as the previous
> assessment centre, but with double the staff, and huge
> maintenance costs, and it is unlikely that the borough will
> allow such an expensive procedure to continue forever."

December 3, 1978

Dear Jerry:

   ... Things have really changed drastically since you were
here. I don't know where to begin. We are all installed
in (Queen's Road), but it's been a pretty dreadful
experience. As a result, we only have one unit out of three
(that were intended for the new facility) functioning, the
rest of the kids have ended up in secure units (locked
units) everyone including (the superintendent) is regularly
off nick (out of sorts). Shawn and Ronald (two of the staff
at Oxford) have left, Alec is now Placement Officer, and
Dinny (a CCO at Cambridge) is leaving in January. The
building is as difficult if not more so to work in as we
expected. It's like suffering from claustrophobia and agro-
phobia simultaneously. How do you keep runaway kids in a
sitting room with eleven exits from it? Nothing is
contained. Any trouble and there is no confrontation ...
the kid is just off (runs away)! We've tried running the
two units as one, the units separately, and now we're down
to just one.
   There has been a lot of violence and damage to property,
and it's hard to know whether we're getting a tougher kind
of kid, whether we're not as skilled as before, or whether
it's the building. But it's now an adolescent unit, and
all of the kids are between 13 and 16 years old.
   Things are quite active in the rest of the borough also.
The residential workers are getting militant. (One of the
centers) has been on strike for 8 weeks.... We've had
pickets and are going to refuse admission of any kid.

We can see from these letters that all of the problems associated
with the move and discussed throughout the book have indeed
materialized. There were also developments that were not anticipated. For example, one large family of children that had
formally been split between Oxford and Cambridge had apparently
been moved to a single unit elsewhere (the one noted above)
causing an 8-week strike. The strike at this facility was
spreading by way of pickets to other assessment centers. The
staff at Queen's Road we are told, was about to refuse new
admissions in a sympathy move. A number of staff at Oxford and
some from Cambridge quit upon moving to Queen's Road. Some of
these workers were relatively new, others were long-time members
of staff. The age composition of the children has changed, they
are now all between 13 and 16. The initiation of locked units
for the first time to deal with the containment problem resulted
in more children being transferred to other institutions. Among

these, there was a marked increase in the number of children being routed into psychiatric care. The consultant tells us: "It is difficult to know whether the building or the set up was driving them (the children) crazy or whether this was the way that the staff were trying to use the psychiatrists to get rid of difficult children." The consequences for childcare in either case is clear. The move to the new facility has lead to an even more precipitous slide in the quality of care at the assessment center. It is also interesting to note that in the consultant's opinion it is not this poor level of care that the borough is unlikely to allow to continue, but the expenses that it entails. If the consultants and staff were unable to dissuade Social Services from proceeding with the project, the weight of the British pound might.

I think it is fair to say that with the move to the new facility, things were not as bad as the RCCOs had anticipated, they were worse. It now takes twice the staff to handle the same number of children as before, not to mention the astronomical cost of maintenance. In fact, it is uncanny how accurate the staff has been in their prediction of things to come. Some of this Notradamus-like ability can be attributed to a self-fulfilling prophesy, i.e., the staff anticipated certain negative conse-quences in the move, and having finally arrived at the new site, lived out their anxieties. While this may have been partially true and contributed to an already bad situation, the problems of containment resolved through lock-ups was real; property damage was real; the mass exodus of disenchanted workers was real; the institutional qualities and procedures within the new facility were real; and so on. Indeed, one must conclude that the move was a bad move, and that this was so not only because of staff "negativism", but for the reasons noted above.

TOTAL INSTITUTIONS: A REASSESSMENT OF "HOUSES" AND "HOMES"

We have discussed in the preceding chapters some of the reasons why Oxford and Cambridge were destined to remain houses, but not homes, notwithstanding the good intentions and efforts of the staff. Many of the staff, while they worked to make a home within "the house" knew this. Indeed, some were ambivalent about initiating this first step in the placement process for the child.

These childcare officers were convinced that the child was
better off at home, no matter how deprived an environment that
might have been, given the availability of "real" options for
"care". The reasons for this were numerous. As previously
noted, CCOs never heard of one of their wards becoming a member
of Parliament, only convicted felons; they themselves had, in
some cases, experienced poverty or "broken homes" and could
relate to the children's problems. Staff felt that placing the
child in the Center for assessment, obtaining a Care Order, and
dictating terms to the parents all undermined the parent's
already weakened position, and did little to reunite the family.
There was no hard evidence to indicate that children placed in
care faired better than those in similar circumstances who
weren't; and CCOs knew firsthand how poor the care was in long-
stay facilities (one member of staff was himself a product of
such an environment).

The above situation led to a serious dilemma. First, to hold
to this position meant that the entire assessment process was
"academic", because whatever one uncovered about the family
dynamics, the child was better off at home. Given this, there
was no point to reception and assessment centers or the work
of CCOs. Taken seriously, such a position would have made the
role of residential childcare officer "redundant".

This was in fact the position of the key consultant. His
contention was that it was in the best interest of the child to
identify problem families and then bring family therapy to the
child and family, rather than bring the family to the service.
Such preventative "outreach" work would result (in his view) in
fewer cases of family problems, fewer problem children, fewer
referrals to care settings, a reduced expenditure in public
funds and a series of other beneficial effects that would in
the long run be felt throughout the community. In this plan,
CCOs would be trained and used as para-professionals in outreach
programs operating out of small units (houses) throughout the
borough. These recommendations were not idle thoughts, but were
presented to the Social Services as alternatives in written
position papers. Thus far, these recommendations have fallen
on deaf ears. I feel this is unfortunate. It is the author's
belief that they warrant a serious hearing. There are inherent
reasons why settings like Oxford and Cambridge and those of the
new assessment center tend to produce more problems than they
eliminate. Some of these reasons were astutely noted by Goffman
in his formulation of "Total Institutions".[2]

Goffman notes five groupings of total institution. First are
institutions established for the care of persons felt to be both
incapable and harmless, such as homes for the blind, aged,
orphaned and indigent. Second are places established to care
for persons felt to be both incapable of looking after themselves
and a threat to the community, albeit an unintended one, e.g.,
TB sanitaria or mental hospitals. Third is a type of total
institution organized to protect the community against what are
felt to be intentional dangers, where the welfare of those
constrained are not the immediate issue: jails, penitentiaries,
or concentration camps. Fourth are institutions supposedly
established to better pursue some instrumental task, e.g., army
barracks, ships, boarding schools, or work camps. Finally there
are those settings designed as retreats from the world and
training centers for the faithful, e.g., abbeys, monasteries,
or convents.

Having provided a rough grouping of the types of total institutions, we will now go on to consider some of their special
characteristics. First and foremost is the fact that the
person constrained (the inmate) sleeps, plays, and works in the
same place. Secondly, their time is scheduled and routinized
for the convenience of the staff. Third, there are three main
statuses within total institutional settings: inmate, staff,
and administrator. Inmates have little if any control of the
course of their lives while institutionalized, while staff and
administrators have all. Fourth, the inmate is subject to a
series of degradations, humiliations, and abasements of self
in an effort on staff's part to have him forego the ways of the
"outside" world and accept the ways of institution. Fifth,
these two worlds are not only different, but antagonistic in
principle. For example, outside one schedules his own time to
a large extent, is insured some privacy, usually works, plays,
and sleeps in different places; reads, eats, and does as he
likes and comes and goes as he pleases.

Allowing that the "outside" is like the "inside" in that
citizens are also constrained in their behavior in certain ways
(indeed society is contingent upon these constraints) the extent
and nature of these constraints are qualitatively different for
the inmate. In fact, being an inmate usually means that one
has lost one's civilian status and with it its rights and
privileges.

The question presents itself, how can being an unwilling party
to such an arrangement result in the inmate's rehabilitation,
when everything that goes on "within" is opposite to that which

goes on "without"? Indeed, the better one becomes "adjusted"
to the "inside", the worse one is adjusted to the "outside", by
definition. The children at the reception and assessment center
were subject to many of the features outlined above.

Goffman notes in another work that one does not always take
kindly to society's efforts to "cool" us out of old and into
new status that are a normal part of the life cycle.[3] How much
more reluctant inmates are to accept the perverse forms of
socialization that go with confinement is given by the fact that
prison guards, ward attendants, and military police are there
not so much to keep outsiders from getting in as to ensure that
insiders do not get out. The same was true of course of childcare officers. We have already discussed the problem of
containment.

Given the above, one can only wonder how childcare facilities
(full of captive audiences) can hope to succeed in providing
the child with a more "normal" environment and thereby help
ready him for a successful re-entry into "outside" life. Quite
apart from the good intentions of the staff in the best of all
possible "inside" worlds, the formal features of total institutions (some of which were outlined above) seem destined to
subvert these efforts.

With this in mind, and until there is some real ground for
believing that childcare facilities provide a more meaningful
and constructive environment inside than the child could
possibly get outside, and that such settings are truly "in the
child's best interests", I think we would do well to reappraise
the expansion of such agencies at the expense of reasonable,
but untried alternatives.

Notes

Chapter 1

1. For a discussion of others seen on a "revolving door" basis by Social Services, see Jerry Jacobs, "Symbolic Bureaucracy", A Case Study of a Social Welfare Agency", *Social Forces*, <u>47</u>(4), June 1969, pp. 413-433.

Chapter 2

1. Brendan Behan, *Borstal Boy*, London: Huchinson, 1958.
2. For a discussion of the need for stability and continuity as well as innovation and change within a formal organizational structure, see Peter M. Blau, *Dynamics of Bureaucracy*, Chicago: University of Chicago Press, 1955, pp. 183-200.
3. The author has worked as a medical sociologist in two major mental hospital settings in the United States for a total of 5 years and visited many others, and can only say that the social and physical environment at Oxford was far superior to anything I have seen in U.S. mental hospitals. In fact, my impressions of Oxford are very different from Philip's in that regard, but very similar in others.

Chapter 3

1. A "gatekeeper" is a key "inside" person who introduces and vouches for some "outsider", so that the outsider can gain access to inside information and understandings within the group he seeks to study.
2. This mode is frequently portrayed in police work. The analogy between CCOs and the police is an apt one in other regards. Both are obliged to deal with enforcing rules, catching and punishing violators, and problems of containment.

3. W.I. Thomas, *The Child in America*, New York: Knopf, 1928, p. 572.

4. "Consciousness of Kind" was a term used by Franklin H. Giddens. For a discussion see A. Small, "Fifty Years of Sociology in the United States", *A.J.S.* 1-52, 1916.

5. For a discussion of "double bind", see Gregory Bateson *et al.*, "Toward a Theory of Schizophrenia" in *Behavioral Science*, 1, No. 4, 251-264.

6. Jay Haley in describing the role of the righteous mother in the schizophrenic family notes that: "Schizophrenia is sometimes called the disease of Christianity. The early Christians could not be easily opposed since they insisted that whatever they did was for your sake and if you wished to harm them they would only turn the other cheek and make you feel guilty." The author would suggest that "paranoid" parents were in much the same situation *vis-à-vis* the agency.
   Jay Haley, "Whither Family Therapy" in *Families in Crisis*, Paul & Lois Glasser editors, New York: Harper & Row, 1970, p. 190.

Chapter 4

1. For a discussion of "Glosses", see Harold Garfinkel, *Studies in Ethonomethodology*, New Jersey: Prentice-Hall, 1967, p. 33.

2. For a discussion of opinion leaders, see Paul Lazersfeld, "The Process of Opinion and Attitude Formation", in the *Language of Social Research*, by Paul Lazersfeld *et al.*, New York: The Free Press, 1962, pp. 231-242.

3. For the role of jury foreman, see Fred L. Strodtbeck *et al.*, "Social Status in Jury Deliberations" in *A.S.R.* 22 (December 1957), 713-19.

4. For a discussion of how psychiatrists are the real decision-makers within the "Therapeutic Community", see Mark Lefton *et al.*, "Decision Making in a Mental Hospital: Real, Perceived, and Ideal", *A.S.R.* 24 (1959), 822-829.

5. For a discussion of negotiating reality, see Stanford M. Lyman and Marvin B. Scott, *A Sociology of the Absurd*, New York, Appleton-Century-Cropts, 1970, pp. 1-28.

6. I am indebted to Howard Schwartz for some of the ideas incorporated in this discussion. To see how and why, the reader is referred to his article "On Recognizing Mistakes: A Case of Practical Reasoning in Psychotherapy", in *Qualitative Sociology: A Method to the Madness*, by Howard Schwartz and Jerry Jacobs, New York: The Free Press, 1979, pp. 405-17.

7.   W.I. Thomas, *The Child in America*, New York: Knopf, 1928, p. 584.

8.   For a critique of this position, see Jerry Jacobs, *Adolescent Suicide*, New York, John Wiley & Sons, 1974, pp. 83-86.

9.   For a psychiatric treatment of "broken homes", "early childhood trauma", and "maternal deprivation", and how they predispose to depression and suicide in later life, see Theodore L. Dorpat *et al.*, "Broken Homes and Attempted and Completed Suicide", *Archives of General Psychiatry*, X11 (February 1965), pp. 213-216.

10.   Edwin Lement, "Paranoia and the Dynamics of Exclusion", *Sociometry*, 25, No. 1 (March 1962), pp. 1-20.

Chapter 6

1.   From Steven Marcus, "Their Brothers Keepers: An Episode from English History", in *Doing Good: The Limits of Benevolence*, by Williard Gaylin *et al.*, New York: Pantheon Books, 1978, p. 66.

2.   For a discussion of Total Institutions, see Erving Goffman, *Asylums*, New York: Anchor Books, 1961, pp. 1-124.

3.   Erving Goffman, "On Cooling the Mark Out", *Psychiatry* (November 1952), p. 451.